What to Say When Someone Dies

EULOGY *Writing*

The Complete Handbook to Help You Craft Compassionate and Heartfelt Eulogies

Christian Funeral and Memorial Services

Jason A. Solomon, B.Ed.

Dedication

To all who have stood before family, friends, and congregations to speak words of love, remembrance, and faith, may this book serve as a guiding light in your time of need.

To those who grieve, may you find comfort in knowing that love never fades, and that in Christ, we have the promise of eternal life.

"To be absent from the body is to be present with the Lord." - 2 Corinthians 5:8

This book is dedicated to the memory of those who have gone before us, and to the voices that honour their legacy. May the words within bring peace, strength, and the assurance that love endures beyond this life.

Bonus Resource – Eulogy Writing AI

As a special bonus, I want to share something that may help you when words feel hardest to find. There may come a time when you are asked to speak at a funeral or memorial, standing before family and friends to honour someone you loved. It is a moment full of emotion, where memory and loss collide, and many people struggle to know where to begin. To support you in such times, I created EULOGYWRITING.AI - a compassionate tool that helps you turn personal memories into a warm, authentic tribute.

By sharing a few details - stories, habits, quirks, and moments that mattered - the tool gently guides you into shaping a meaningful draft you can refine in your own voice. It is simple, private, and there to walk with you when you need it most.

To use this bonus resource, simply scan the QR code provided in this book or visit the page directly at:

https://eulogywriting.ai

Every life deserves to be remembered with words that last, and I hope this gift helps you when you need it most.

Scan the QR code to access the AI Tool

Copyright

© 2025 Jason A Solomon. All rights reserved. No part of this book may be copied, stored, or transmitted by any means - electronic, mechanical, photocopying, recording, or otherwise - without the prior written permission of the publisher, except in the case of brief quotations for the purpose of critical review. Unauthorized distribution or reproduction of this book is strictly prohibited. The author has made every effort to ensure the accuracy of the information presented, but neither the author nor the publisher assumes responsibility for errors or omissions.

Disclaimer

This book is intended as a guide to assist in writing and delivering eulogies. While every effort has been made to provide meaningful and respectful content, the examples and templates within are fictional and should not be considered representations of real individuals or events. Any resemblance to actual persons, living or deceased, is purely coincidental. The information provided is for general reference and should not replace professional or religious counsel. Readers are encouraged to tailor their eulogies to reflect personal relationships, cultural customs, and religious beliefs. The author and publisher assume no responsibility for how the content is used in individual circumstances. This book does not provide legal, medical, or psychological advice. For specific concerns related to grief, loss, or public speaking anxiety, readers are encouraged to seek guidance from qualified professionals.

Post a Review

Thank you for allowing this book to be a part of your journey. It was written with the hope of providing guidance, comfort, and inspiration during one of life's most profound moments. If this book has helped in any way, please consider leaving a review on Amazon.

Your feedback not only helps others understand the value of this resource but also ensures that more people find the support they need in crafting a meaningful eulogy.

With gratitude and blessings, - Jason A. Solomon

FOREWORD

Writing and delivering a eulogy is a responsibility that often arrives unannounced, in a moment when grief feels overwhelming and words seem insufficient. I never imagined that I would stand before so many grieving families, called upon to give voice to their memories, their sorrow, and their love. Yet, over the years, I found myself stepping up when others could not, offering words when emotions were too raw for my family members to speak.

The first eulogy I delivered was for my younger brother, taken from us far too soon in a tragic car accident at the age of 18. The weight of grief bore heavily on my family, and my siblings were unable to find the strength to speak. As a teacher accustomed to standing before students, I thought I might manage the task, though nothing could have prepared me for the depth of emotion that came with it. I knew that my words had to capture his essence - his humour, his spirit, the moments that defined him - not just for me but for those who mourned alongside me.

That experience led to another, and then another. When my uncle passed after a battle with cancer, his sons - both older than me - struggled to find the words to say goodbye. My aunt approached me with a request: Would I do the honour of speaking for him? I hesitated, uncertain if I could adequately convey a life filled with love, humour, and resilience. But I saw the comfort my words had brought to my brother's service, and I knew I had to try.

Years later, my father passed suddenly from a stroke. Once again, my family looked to me to speak on their behalf. With nearly 300 people gathered to honour his life, I felt the familiar weight of responsibility settle upon me. I spoke of his strength, his unwavering love, and the lessons he instilled in us. It was one of the hardest things I have ever done, but I understood that these words - spoken through tears - were part of his legacy.

In 2022, I delivered my fourth eulogy, this time for another uncle, a man who battled Parkinson's disease with immense courage. His daughters, my cousins, wanted to share their thoughts but found themselves unable to stand before the congregation. Days before the service they handed me their words, their emotions woven into every sentence, trusting me to honour their father's life. I structured their memories into a narrative that flowed naturally, ensuring their love for him was heard and felt by all.

Through these experiences, I came to understand something profound: a eulogy is not just a speech. It is a bridge between the past and the present, a tribute that carries a person's memory forward. It is an acknowledgment of their journey, their impact, and the love they leave behind.

"A lasting memory"

This book exists because I know firsthand how difficult it is to write and deliver a eulogy. In the depths of grief, clarity can be elusive, and the fear of not doing justice to a loved one's memory can be paralysing. I have written this book to provide guidance, to help those who find themselves in the same position I once did - searching for the right words in a moment of sorrow.

You will find prewritten eulogies in these pages, structured to offer comfort, honour, and sincerity. Each can be used as it is or adapted to reflect your unique connection to the person you are remembering. Guide markers have been included to help you personalize each speech, making it a truly heartfelt tribute. I encourage you to infuse these words with your own memories, your own reflections, and your own emotions. Most importantly, remember that there is no perfect eulogy - only an honest one. Speak from the heart, and you will honour their legacy in the most meaningful way possible.

It is my hope that this book serves as both a source of comfort and a practical tool, helping you navigate one of life's most difficult moments with grace and confidence.

Jason A. Solomon

Contents

Foreword *7*

Introduction *13*

Part 1: My Story – Delivering Eulogies at Family Funerals **16**

My Journey in Delivering Eulogies *17*

Preparing for Each Eulogy *20*

The Emotional Experience of Delivering a Eulogy *24*

Lessons Learned and Advice for Others *28*

Part 2: Understanding Eulogies **33**

The Meaning and Importance of Eulogies *34*

The Structure of a Meaningful Eulogy *37*

Delivering Your Eulogy with Confidence *42*

Part 3: Heartfelt Eulogy Examples by Age **47**

For Newborn and Infants (0– 1 Year Old) *48*

For Young Children (Ages 1-6) *52*

For Children (Ages 7-12) *56*

For Teens and Young Adults (Ages 13-21) *60*

For Spouses and Partners *66*

For Parents and Grandparents *73*

For Siblings and Close Friends *81*

For Unexpected or Tragic Deaths 91

For Death Due to Illness 96

For the Elderly Who Lived a Full Life 101

For Public Figures and Community Leaders 111

Part 4: Christian Faith and Eulogies 118

Incorporating Christianity into A Eulogy 119

Bible Verses for Writing Your Eulogy 124

Part 5: Additional Guidance & Resources 129

Handling Grief and Loss 130

Funeral Etiquette and Typical Traditions 136

Part 5: Additional Guidance & Resources 141

Writing a Personalized Eulogy from Scratch 142

Final Thoughts: The Power of Words in Remembrance 147

Appendix: Bonus Material 151

Thesaurus for Eulogy Writing 164

Example Eulogies for Writing Guidance 170

Notes 203

INTRODUCTION

The Purpose of This Book

The passing of a loved one is an incredibly emotional and challenging time, and finding the right words to honour their memory can feel overwhelming. Many people struggle with writing a eulogy, either due to grief, lack of experience, or fear of public speaking. This book serves as a guide to help individuals prepare and deliver a heartfelt, meaningful eulogy with confidence. By providing prewritten eulogies and practical advice, this book offers support to those who need it most during a difficult moment in life.

This collection of eulogies has been thoughtfully designed to cover various circumstances, from the loss of a parent, sibling, or child to the passing of a close friend or community leader. Whether you choose to use these eulogies as they are or modify them to include personal anecdotes and memories, the goal remains the same: to honour and celebrate the life of the deceased in a way that brings comfort to those left behind.

Why Eulogies Matter: Honouring a Life

A eulogy is more than just a speech; it is a tribute to a life lived, a reflection of the impact someone has had on others, and a way to provide comfort and closure to those grieving. It allows us to share cherished memories, express our love and gratitude, and acknowledge the profound influence of the departed on our lives.

Through stories and reflections, eulogies remind us that a person's legacy extends far beyond their time on earth. It is through these words that we keep their memory alive, sharing their values, lessons, and the joy they brought into the world.

A well-delivered eulogy can bring a sense of peace and unity to those gathered. It offers an opportunity to reflect, to laugh through the tears, and to find solace in knowing that a loved one's life was meaningful and appreciated.

How to Use This Book

This book has been structured to provide both guidance and practical tools for delivering a eulogy. It is divided into several sections to help you find what you need quickly:

- **Understanding Eulogies** – This section provides insight into the structure of a eulogy, tips on writing and delivering one, and the importance of tone and pacing.
- **Prewritten Eulogies** – Organized by category, these eulogies can be used as they are or modified to reflect personal memories and anecdotes.
- **Christian Faith and Eulogies** – This section includes Bible verses, prayers, and religious elements that can be incorporated into a eulogy.
- **Additional Resources** – Helpful information on handling grief, funeral etiquette, and strategies for overcoming public speaking anxiety.
- **Thesaurus for Eulogy Writing** – A curated list of words and phrases to help personalize and enhance your tribute.

You may choose to read this book cover to cover, or you may use it as a reference guide, selecting sections that are most relevant to your situation. Whether you need inspiration, structure, or reassurance, this book is here to help.

Personalizing a Prewritten Eulogy

While this book provides structured eulogies, it is essential to make them personal. A eulogy should reflect the unique life and character of the deceased, bringing their memory to life through stories, personality traits, and shared experiences. Here are some ways to personalize a eulogy:

- o **Insert Names and Specific Memories** – Replace generic references with the name of the person you are honouring and add specific anecdotes that illustrate their personality and values.

- o **Incorporate Humour and Sentiment** – A well-balanced eulogy can include both heartfelt and light-hearted moments, reflecting the individual's spirit and the joy they brought to others.

- o **Use Guide Markers** – Throughout the eulogy templates, placeholders such as **[Insert Name]** and **[Include a Personal Memory]** etc, will prompt you to add meaningful details.

- o **Adjust Tone and Language** – Modify the wording to align with your personal style and the nature of the funeral service, whether formal, casual, or deeply religious.

Remember, the most powerful eulogies come from the heart. Even if you choose to use a prewritten speech, making it personal will create a more profound and meaningful tribute.

Part 1: My Story – Delivering Eulogies at Family Funerals

Chapter 1

MY JOURNEY IN DELIVERING EULOGIES

How I Came to Deliver Four Eulogies at Family Funerals

The role of delivering a eulogy is not something I ever anticipated, yet it became a defining part of my journey through grief. I found myself standing before mourners on four separate occasions, tasked with putting into words the emotions that so many struggled to express. Each time, I felt the immense weight of responsibility - to honour, to comfort, and to capture the essence of a life well lived.

It began with my younger brother. He was taken from us suddenly, at just 18 years old, in a tragic car accident. When the time came to speak at his funeral, my siblings were overcome with grief, unable to stand before the gathered family and friends. Though I had never delivered a eulogy before, I knew that someone needed to speak for him. My experience as a teacher had given me some comfort with public speaking, but nothing could prepare me for the depth of emotion I felt when I took my place before the congregation.

The First Eulogy: My Younger Brother's Sudden Passing

The shock of losing my younger brother "Nathan" was unlike anything I had ever experienced. Writing his eulogy was painful -

each word felt like a fresh wound, but I knew it had to be done. I wanted his friends and family to remember him for his humour, his kindness, and the way he made us all laugh. I infused the eulogy with personal anecdotes, stories that reflected his mischievous spirit, and the love we all had for him. When I stood before the crowd, my heart pounded, my throat tightened, but I spoke. And as I spoke, I felt his presence in the laughter and the tears that followed.

The Challenge of Speaking for My Uncle's Funeral

Just months after my brother's passing, my uncle "Albert" succumbed to cancer. His two sons, both older than me, struggled to find the words to say goodbye. My aunt approached me with a request - to speak on their behalf. At first, I hesitated, uncertain if I could shoulder this responsibility again. But I realized that my words at my brother's funeral had offered comfort, and perhaps, I could do the same for my uncle's family. I spoke of the gatherings he had loved, the humour he brought to our lives, and the quiet strength he showed even in his final days.

The Emotional Weight of Eulogizing My Father

Years later, my father "John" passed away suddenly from a stroke. The room was filled with nearly 300 people, all there to honour him. Once again, my family looked to me to speak. This time, it was different. I wasn't just speaking for him - I was speaking for myself. I spoke about his resilience, his sacrifices, and the lessons he had imparted to me. It was one of the hardest things I have ever done, pausing multiple times to steady my voice, to push through the overwhelming wave of grief. But in that moment, I understood what a eulogy truly was - a bridge between memories and farewell.

The Responsibility of Delivering My Final Eulogy for My Uncle in 2022

In 2022, I was once again asked to stand before a grieving family and offer words of remembrance. This time, it was for my uncle "Verdon", who had battled Parkinson's disease for years. His daughters, my cousins, had so much to say but could not summon the strength to stand before the congregation. They handed me their words, their emotions woven into each sentence, and entrusted me with their father's memory. I structured their memories into a flowing narrative, ensuring that his love, faith, and dedication to his family were heard and felt by all.

At the wake, my cousins approached me and joked, "You're hired." It was a moment of levity in a day of sorrow, but it reinforced something I had come to realize - delivering a eulogy is not about performance, nor about formality. It is about connection. It is about ensuring that those gathered find comfort in knowing that their loved one's story was told, their presence acknowledged, and their impact remembered.

Each of these eulogies shaped my understanding of loss, grief, and the power of words. They are why this book exists - to help others navigate the immense responsibility of delivering a eulogy when the moment arises.

This Eulogy for my uncle "Verdon" can be found in the *Appendix* section of this book. With the expressed permission of his wife Shirley and two daughters Nerida and Amanda. Their contribution to this book is greatly appreciated.

PREPARING FOR EACH EULOGY

The Approach to Structuring Each Eulogy

Writing a eulogy is both an honour and a responsibility. It requires careful thought, a deep understanding of the person being remembered, and an awareness of the emotions of those in mourning. Over the years, I developed an approach to structuring eulogies that allowed me to craft meaningful and engaging tributes:

- **Opening – Setting the Tone**: A gentle introduction that acknowledges the loss while setting a tone that reflects the personality of the deceased. Whether solemn, light-hearted, or a blend of both, this introduction sets the stage.
- **Personal Stories and Reflections**: The heart of the eulogy, this section brings the departed's personality, values, and impact to life through anecdotes and memories.
- **Acknowledging the Grief and Offering Comfort**: Recognizing the pain of loss and providing words of solace to the grieving family and friends.
- **A Closing Message**: A final farewell that encapsulates the essence of the individual and leaves the audience with a message of remembrance and gratitude.

While this structure provides a foundation, each eulogy is unique, shaped by the life and legacy of the person being honoured.

Writing from the Heart vs. Following a Structured Format

One of the greatest challenges in preparing a eulogy is deciding whether to write freely from the heart or adhere to a structured format. In my experience, a combination of both works best.

Writing from the heart ensures authenticity. Speaking in the first person and sharing personal reflections make the eulogy genuine and relatable. However, structure provides clarity, guiding the audience through the emotions and memories without feeling disjointed or overwhelming.

For my brother's eulogy, I wrote freely, allowing emotions to guide my words. For my uncle's eulogy, I followed a more structured approach, incorporating memories from his daughters in a cohesive narrative. Both approaches were equally effective because they honoured the unique relationships and experiences we shared.

Finding the Right Balance Between Humour, Reflection, and Reverence

A well-crafted eulogy should evoke emotions that reflect the life of the deceased. Striking the right balance between humour, reflection, and reverence is essential.

Humour, when used appropriately, can provide warmth and comfort. It reminds us of the joy and laughter our loved ones brought into our lives. In my brother's eulogy, I shared stories of his playful antics, which brought smiles to the faces of his grieving friends.

Reflection allows us to explore the deeper impact of their presence in our lives - the lessons they taught us, the moments that defined them. And reverence ensures that the eulogy maintains the dignity and honour the occasion demands.

Each eulogy requires a tailored balance. Too much solemnity can make it heavy and difficult for listeners, while too much humour can seem out of place. The key is to be authentic and consider what the departed would have wanted their loved ones to remember.

How Family Involvement Shaped Each Eulogy

Every eulogy I have delivered was shaped, in part, by the family members of the deceased. Gathering memories and insights from others provided a more comprehensive view of the person's life, allowing me to create a eulogy that resonated with everyone in attendance.

For my father's eulogy, I spoke to my siblings about his strengths and challenges, ensuring his legacy was honoured from multiple perspectives. For my uncle, his daughters provided me with stories they wished to include which I wove into a structured and heartfelt speech. The collective memories of family members helped me capture not just the facts of their lives, but the depth of their influence and love.

The Role of Faith and Spirituality in My Writing

Faith played a varying role in the eulogies I delivered, depending on the beliefs of the deceased and their families. Some eulogies contained little to no religious references, while others included biblical passages, prayers, and references to faith as a source of comfort.

For my brother, who was not religious, I focused on the love and connections he built in his short life. For my uncle, a devout Presbyterian, I incorporated scripture and reflections on faith to honour his beliefs. When I eulogized my father, I included subtle religious elements to respect his upbringing, while allowing space for those in the congregation who were not as spiritually inclined.

Faith and spirituality can provide profound comfort in times of grief, but they must be included with thoughtfulness and sensitivity. Regardless of religious affiliation, every eulogy should aim to provide peace, unity, and a sense of closure to those mourning.

Preparing a eulogy is an emotional, deeply personal process. By blending structure with heartfelt expression, balancing humour with reverence, including the voices of family members, and incorporating faith when appropriate, we create eulogies that truly honour the lives of those we have lost.

> Each word, each memory, and each pause in a eulogy carries meaning, allowing us to transform grief into a shared celebration of a life well-lived.

Chapter 3

THE EMOTIONAL EXPERIENCE OF DELIVERING A EULOGY

Managing Emotions While Writing and Delivering a Eulogy

Writing a eulogy is an emotionally charged process. It forces us to reflect deeply on our relationship with the deceased, often stirring up memories that bring both comfort and sorrow. While preparing a eulogy, it is natural to experience waves of grief, but it is important to allow these emotions to guide rather than overwhelm the writing process.

One of the most effective ways to manage emotions while writing is to take breaks when needed. There were times when I had to step away, collect my thoughts, and return with a clearer mind. Writing in stages helped me maintain composure, allowing me to refine my words while ensuring that my emotions did not cloud the message I wanted to convey.

Delivering the eulogy, however, presents a different challenge. Standing before a grieving audience can be daunting, especially when emotions threaten to take over. To manage this, I found it helpful to focus on breathing deeply, speaking slowly, and pausing when necessary. If overwhelmed, allowing a brief moment of silence is perfectly acceptable - it gives the audience time to reflect and allows the speaker to regain composure.

Coping with Overwhelming Grief While Speaking

Despite preparation, emotions can surface unexpectedly when delivering a eulogy. Even experienced speakers can find themselves struggling with tears or a wavering voice. Coping with grief while speaking requires both mental and physical strategies.

- o **Acknowledge the Emotion** – It is okay to express grief while speaking. A slight pause or moment of reflection can be powerful and relatable to the audience.

- o **Use Supportive Anchors** – Looking at a familiar and supportive face in the audience can provide strength. Alternatively, focusing on a fixed point in the room can help maintain composure.

- o **Have a Glass of Water Nearby** – Taking a sip of water can provide a momentary break and help steady the voice.

- o **Practice Reading Aloud Beforehand** – Familiarity with the words can reduce the likelihood of being caught off guard by emotions during the speech.

- o **Remember the Purpose** – Keeping in mind that the eulogy is a gift to the deceased and those grieving can help shift focus from personal grief to honouring the individual's life.

The most meaningful eulogies are those that are spoken from the heart, and emotions are a natural part of that. There is no need to apologize for grief - it is a testament to love and remembrance.

The Importance of Audience Connection and Reading Reactions

A eulogy is not just about speaking; it is about connecting. The emotions of those in attendance will vary - some will cry, others will smile at fond memories, and many will simply listen in quiet reflection. Understanding the audience's emotions and responding to them can make a eulogy even more impactful.

- o **Engage with the Audience** – Making eye contact, even briefly, creates a sense of connection. It reassures those present that the words being spoken come from a place of sincerity.

- o **Acknowledge Shared Emotions** – If the audience responds with tears, a pause allows them to process their emotions. If they laugh at a humorous memory, embracing the shared moment can bring warmth and comfort.

- o **Speak with Authenticity** – There is no need to deliver a eulogy in a formal, robotic manner. Speaking naturally, as though in a heartfelt conversation, makes it more relatable and engaging.

> Observing audience reactions can help adjust the delivery in real time, ensuring that the message resonates with those in mourning.

Adjusting the Tone, Pace, and Delivery Based on the Congregation's Response

Delivering a eulogy requires flexibility. Each audience and setting is different, and being attuned to the energy in the room can guide adjustments in tone, pace, and delivery.

- **Tone**: If the audience is solemn and reflective, a calm and measured tone may be more appropriate. If there are moments of light-heartedness, allowing a smile or a softer tone can provide balance.

- **Pace**: Speaking too quickly can make it difficult for the audience to absorb the words, while speaking too slowly can make the eulogy feel drawn out. A steady, deliberate pace with intentional pauses allows for emphasis and reflection.

- **Delivery**: If the audience seems particularly emotional, allowing moments of silence can provide space for them to process their grief. Conversely, if the atmosphere is tense, a comforting or reassuring statement can help bring a sense of peace.

Adapting to the moment ensures that the eulogy remains engaging and meaningful, creating a lasting tribute that resonates with those in attendance.

Delivering a eulogy is one of the most emotionally challenging experiences a person can face. By managing emotions, allowing oneself to grieve naturally, connecting with the audience, and adjusting the delivery as needed, it becomes possible to honour the deceased in a way that is both heartfelt and memorable. The goal is not perfection - it is sincerity, reflection, and the acknowledgment of a life well-lived.

Chapter 4

LESSONS LEARNED AND ADVICE FOR OTHERS

How These Experiences Changed My View on Eulogies

Before delivering my first eulogy, I thought of them as formal, scripted speeches - necessary but impersonal. However, after standing before grieving families multiple times, I came to understand that a eulogy is far more than a simple farewell. It is an opportunity to bring a person's essence to life through words, to celebrate their joys, acknowledge their struggles, and ensure their impact is remembered.

Eulogies are not about perfection; they are about connection. Each time I stood at a podium, I realized that the people listening were not expecting grand eloquence or flawless delivery - they were seeking comfort, familiarity, and authenticity. A well-crafted eulogy brings unity, allowing mourners to reflect on shared memories and feel that their loved one's life was honoured in a meaningful way.

These experiences have profoundly reshaped my perspective. I now see eulogies as healing tools - not just for those who listen, but for those who speak. They allow us to process grief, express gratitude, and share in collective mourning, reminding us that no one is truly gone as long as their story is told.

The Importance of Speaking from the Heart

One of the greatest lessons I have learned is that sincerity always resonates more than formality. People may not remember every word of a eulogy, but they will remember how it made them feel. Speaking from the heart is the key to crafting a eulogy that is both moving and memorable.

- o **Be Genuine**: Authenticity is more powerful than the most polished speech. Speak as though you are having a heartfelt conversation with the audience rather than delivering a performance.

- o **Share Real Stories**: Personal anecdotes and cherished moments make a eulogy unique. They create a connection between the speaker, the audience, and the memory of the deceased.

- o **Allow Emotion to Show**: Holding back tears or trying to sound overly composed can make a eulogy feel distant. Emotion is natural and, when expressed in balance, can be incredibly moving.

> A eulogy should feel like a final gift to the one who has passed - a tribute that captures their spirit, personality, and the love they shared with the world.

Practical Strategies for Overcoming Nervousness

Even for experienced speakers, delivering a eulogy can be intimidating. The combination of public speaking and grief makes it one of the most emotionally charged speeches a person may ever give. However, these strategies can help ease nerves:

- **Prepare in Advance** – Writing and reviewing the eulogy multiple times will build familiarity and confidence.

- **Practice Reading Aloud** – Hearing the words spoken helps identify areas that may need adjustments and allows for better flow.

- **Use Breathing Techniques** – Slow, deep breaths before speaking can help calm nerves and steady the voice.

- **Have a Glass of Water Nearby** – A sip of water provides a natural pause and can help manage a dry throat caused by nerves.

- **Use Notes but Avoid Reading Word-for-Word** – Glancing at key points rather than reading verbatim allows for a more natural and engaging delivery.

- **Remember the Purpose** – Focusing on honouring the deceased rather than personal fears shifts the attention from nervousness to the importance of the moment.

How to Pause and Regain Composure When Emotions Take Over

It is inevitable delivering a eulogy will stir emotions, and sometimes they will become overwhelming. Knowing how to pause and regain composure in those moments is crucial.

- **Acknowledge the Emotion**: It's okay to pause and take a breath. If you need a moment, allow yourself to step back mentally and physically.

- **Look at a Supportive Face**: Finding a familiar, reassuring presence in the audience can provide comfort and encouragement.

- **Take a Sip of Water**: This simple action provides a brief, natural break and can help steady emotions.

- **Use Strategic Pauses**: Intentionally incorporating pauses allows both the speaker and the audience time to reflect, process, and regain composure.

- **Shift Focus to the Message**: Remembering why you are speaking and who you are speaking for can provide the strength needed to continue.

> Mourning is deeply personal, and emotions are a natural part of honouring a loved one. Taking the time to steady yourself ensures that you can deliver the message with clarity and sincerity.

The Lifelong Impact of Delivering a Eulogy

Giving a eulogy is an experience that stays with you forever. It is not just a speech - it is a moment of shared humanity, a reflection of love, and an act of service to both the deceased and the living.

Each eulogy I have delivered has left a lasting impact on me. I have felt the profound weight of loss, but I have also witnessed the power of words to bring comfort and healing. I have seen how laughter, tears, and reflection intertwine in a room full of grieving hearts, bringing people together in remembrance and gratitude.

Beyond the funeral, a eulogy can shape the way we carry forward the memory of those we have lost. It helps solidify their place in our lives, reminding us that their influence, wisdom, and love endure beyond their physical presence. For those who find themselves in the position of delivering a eulogy, know this: it is one of the greatest honours you will ever have. Speak with truth, speak with love, and know that your words will be remembered long after they are spoken.

Part 2: Understanding Eulogies

Chapter 5

THE MEANING AND IMPORTANCE OF EULOGIES

The Role of a Eulogy in a Funeral or Memorial Service

A eulogy serves as a final tribute to a loved one, a moment to honour their life and the impact they had on those around them. It is more than just a speech - it reflects the deceased's character, accomplishments, and the love they shared with family and friends. Whether delivered by a family member, friend, or clergy, a eulogy creates a space where memories are revisited, grief is acknowledged, and the person's essence is celebrated.

Eulogies hold a unique place in funeral and memorial services because they personalize the occasion. While religious readings, music, and rituals offer comfort, the eulogy gives a direct and intimate voice to the departed's story. It allows mourners to connect emotionally, recalling cherished moments, shared laughter, and lessons learned. By hearing a heartfelt eulogy, those in attendance can find solace in the reminder that the person they loved was deeply valued and will not be forgotten.

Providing Comfort to Mourners

Grief can feel isolating, and during the difficult moments of saying goodbye, a well-crafted eulogy provides a sense of unity and collective mourning. It helps attendees process their emotions, offering words that may articulate feelings they struggle to express themselves.

A eulogy can provide comfort in several ways:
- **Validation of Grief** – It acknowledges the deep sorrow felt by those present and reassures them that mourning is a natural response to loss.
- **A Reminder of Love and Connection** – Sharing personal anecdotes and meaningful moments allows mourners to relive the joy and love they experienced with the deceased.
- **Encouragement for Healing** – A well-delivered eulogy does not simply dwell on sadness; it offers hope and a perspective on how the person's legacy will live on in the hearts of those they touched.
- **A Celebration of Life** – While grief is at the heart of a eulogy, it is also an opportunity to celebrate the unique qualities, achievements, and contributions of the deceased.

In times of profound loss, a eulogy reassures mourners that they are not alone in their grief. It reminds them that their loved one's presence lingers in memories, stories, and the bonds they built in life.

Preserving Memories Through Words

A well-crafted eulogy ensures that the story of a loved one's life is remembered and passed on. Words have the power to capture the essence of a person, painting a picture of their kindness, humour, resilience, and passions.

By recounting specific memories, quoting their favourite sayings, or describing their habits and values, a eulogy brings the deceased back to life in the minds of those listening. These shared reflections become touchstones for future generations, ensuring that the person's impact is never forgotten.

Ways to preserve memories through a eulogy include:

- **Personal Anecdotes**: Small, meaningful stories that highlight the person's character and interactions with others.

- **Quotations or Sayings**: Including a favourite phrase, life motto, or words of wisdom they often shared.

- **Descriptive Imagery**: Painting a vivid picture of how they lived, what they loved, and how they made others feel.

- **Messages of Gratitude**: Expressing appreciation for their influence and the love they gave to those around them.

A eulogy is more than just words spoken in a moment of farewell - it is a lasting testament to the life and legacy of a loved one. Through carefully chosen words, we ensure that their memory is honoured, cherished, and carried forward.

Chapter 6

THE STRUCTURE OF A MEANINGFUL EULOGY

Writing a eulogy is a deeply personal and emotional task. It is an opportunity to reflect on a loved one's life, to celebrate their legacy, and to offer comfort to those in mourning. While grief may cloud our ability to find the right words, structuring a eulogy effectively can help guide us through this difficult process. A well-crafted eulogy typically follows a three-part format: the opening, the middle, and the closing. Each section serves a specific purpose in shaping a tribute that is heartfelt, meaningful, and enduring. Whether you choose to speak with solemn reverence, infuse humour into your memories, or draw upon spiritual beliefs, the key is to speak from the heart and honour the individual in a way that resonates with those gathered.

Opening: Setting the Tone

The opening of a eulogy serves as the introduction, setting the tone for the speech and acknowledging the purpose of the gathering. It should be warm, heartfelt, and establish a connection with the audience.

Examples of Different Openings:

- o **Traditional and Respectful** "Good morning, everyone. We are gathered here today to honour and pay tribute to [Name], a person whose kindness, wisdom, and generosity touched so many lives. My name is [Your Name], and it is both a privilege and a solemn duty to share memories of [Name] today. Though our hearts are heavy with grief, we also reflect on the joy and love that [Name] brought into our world."

- **Light-hearted and Personal** "If there's one thing [Name] taught us, it's that laughter and love go hand in hand. They had a knack for turning even the most mundane moments into something extraordinary. So, while today is difficult, I know [Name] would want us to smile through the tears, share stories, and remember the happiness they brought to all of us."

- **Spiritual and Reflective** "We gather here today not just in mourning but in faith, believing that [Name] has transitioned to a place of eternal peace. As we reflect on their life, let us remember that their spirit continues to live on within us - guiding, comforting, and inspiring us."

- **Emotional and Honest** "It's hard to stand here and find the right words to say about someone so dear to us. No amount of preparation could have made this easier. But if there's one thing I know, it's that [Name] would want us to hold onto love, to cherish the moments we had, and to lean on one another in times of sorrow."

- **Poetic and Metaphorical** "Some people are like the stars - shining brightly, guiding us through life's darkest nights. [Name] was one of those people. Their warmth, wisdom, and unwavering kindness lit up the lives of everyone they touched. Today, though we grieve, we also celebrate the brilliance of their legacy."

- **Reverent and Formal** "Today, we stand together in remembrance of [Name], a person whose presence enriched our lives in countless ways. Though we say goodbye, we do so with gratitude for the love, lessons, and memories they left behind. In the face of loss, we find strength in one another and in the enduring impact of [Name]'s life."

- o **Nostalgic and Sentimental** "It feels impossible to sum up the life of [Name] in just a few words, but if I had to choose one, it would be 'irreplaceable.' They had a way of making everyone feel special, loved, and understood. And while we may no longer hear their voice, their laughter, or their wisdom, their presence will always be felt in our hearts."

Middle: Sharing Memories and Stories

The middle section is the heart of the eulogy. It should capture the essence of the deceased by sharing meaningful memories, personal anecdotes, and reflections on their character.

Examples of Different Middle Sections:

- o **Warm and Nostalgic** – "One of my favourite memories of [Name] was their unwavering ability to turn an ordinary day into something memorable."

- o **Humorous and Endearing** – "If you knew [Name], you knew they had a way with words - and that they never told a story just once."

- o **Inspirational and Reflective** – "[Name] was more than a friend - they were a guide, a mentor, and a rock for so many of us."

- o **Sentimental and Heartfelt** – "One of the things I will always cherish about [Name] was their ability to make everyone feel seen and valued."

- **Family-Oriented and Loving** – "Family meant everything to [Name]. Every holiday, every birthday, every Sunday dinner - it was all about togetherness."
- **Legacy and Impact** – "[Name]'s legacy will be carried forward in every life they touched. Their acts of kindness and generosity will never be forgotten."
- **Anecdotal and Relatable** – "There was never a challenge too big for [Name] to tackle. If something broke, they'd fix it. If someone was struggling, they'd help."
- **Work Ethic and Dedication** – "[Name] had an incredible work ethic. They took pride in everything they did, whether it was their career, their home, or their community."
- **Compassionate and Empathetic** – "What set [Name] apart was their kindness. No matter how busy they were, they always had time for others."
- **Spiritual and Grounded** – "Faith was at the core of [Name]'s life. Their unwavering belief provided strength not only for themselves but for those around them."
- **Adventurous and Passionate** – "[Name] had a spirit of adventure that never dimmed. They embraced life with open arms, always ready for the next experience."

Closing: Offering Comfort and a Final Goodbye

Examples of Different Closings:

- **Traditional and Comforting** – "As we say our final goodbyes, let us hold onto the love, the laughter, and the lessons [Name] gave us."

- o **Hopeful and Uplifting** – "Although today is filled with sorrow, let us leave here not with sadness, but with gratitude."

- o **Faith-Based and Reassuring** – "While we mourn today, we take solace in knowing that [Name] has found eternal peace in the presence of the Lord."

- o **Personal and Direct** – "Goodbye, [Name]. You gave us love, you gave us wisdom, and you gave us moments that we will never forget."

- o **Poetic and Reflective** – "Though the sun has set on [Name]'s time with us, their light remains, shimmering in every story told."

- o **Grateful and Celebratory** – "As we leave here today, let us not only grieve but also celebrate."

- o **Quiet and Reflective** – "Some goodbyes are too difficult for words. So instead, let us sit for a moment in silence."

A well-structured eulogy is a tribute to a life well-lived. By following this format - setting the tone, sharing meaningful memories, and offering comfort and closure - you can create a speech that honours the deceased in a heartfelt and memorable way.

Chapter 7

DELIVERING YOUR EULOGY WITH CONFIDENCE

Writing a heartfelt eulogy is one part of the process, but standing before a room full of mourners to deliver it is another challenge entirely. Public speaking can be daunting under normal circumstances, but when emotions are running high, it becomes even more difficult. However, with thoughtful preparation and a few key strategies, you can deliver a eulogy with clarity, composure, and the heartfelt sincerity your loved one deserves.

Overcoming Nervousness

It is natural to feel nervous before delivering a eulogy. The weight of the moment, combined with the fear of public speaking, can make even the most confident speaker feel anxious. Here are a few ways to manage and overcome nervousness:

- **Acknowledge Your Feelings** – It is perfectly normal to feel anxious. Accepting this can help prevent you from becoming overwhelmed.

- **Practice Aloud** – Reading your eulogy multiple times before the service will help familiarize you with the flow of words and reduce the fear of stumbling.

- **Use Deep Breathing Techniques** – Slow, deep breaths before speaking will help regulate your heart rate and calm your nerves.

- o **Focus on the Message, Not Yourself** – Remember, the purpose of a eulogy is to honour the deceased, not to deliver a flawless performance.
- o **Have a Backup Plan** – If emotions overwhelm you, pause, take a sip of water, and collect yourself. It is okay to take a moment to regain composure.

> I recalled how nervous I was when I delivered my first eulogy for my youngest brother. I had no idea how I would get through it, but I reminded myself that it wasn't about me - it was about honouring him. That shift in my mindset helped me stand in front of the congregation and speak from the heart.

Tips for a Clear and Engaging Delivery

Even the most beautifully written eulogy can lose its impact if it is not delivered effectively. Here are key strategies for ensuring your words are clear, engaging, and meaningful to your audience:

1. Speak Slowly and Clearly

When nervous, it is common to rush through sentences. Slow down, enunciate, and allow each word to be heard. Pausing at natural breaks helps emphasize key points and gives the audience time to absorb your words.

> When I delivered my father's eulogy, I had to pause several times to keep my emotions in check. The silence felt long in my mind, but I realized that those moments of pause allowed everyone to reflect on the words I had just spoken.

2. Make Eye Contact

Glancing up occasionally from your notes to connect with the audience creates a sense of shared remembrance. If direct eye contact is too difficult, looking just above the crowd or at a familiar face for reassurance can help.

Example: While reading Hank's eulogy, I found comfort in looking toward my cousins. Seeing their quiet nods and shared smiles reassured me that I was capturing the essence of who he was.

3. Use a Conversational Tone

A eulogy should feel like a personal tribute rather than a formal speech. Speak naturally, as if you were sharing cherished memories with close friends and family.

> When speaking about Hank's love for storytelling, I used a tone that reflected his own voice - animated and full of warmth. That approach made the eulogy feel more like a conversation rather than a speech. As if was coming from him.

4. Control Your Breathing

Shallow breathing can increase anxiety. Taking slow, deep breaths before and during your speech will help keep your voice steady and clear.

5. Use Notes, But Avoid Reading Word-for-Word

Having a printed copy of your eulogy is helpful but try not to rely on it completely. Reading directly from the page can make the speech feel impersonal. Familiarizing yourself with the structure beforehand allows you to maintain a more natural flow.

> Days before delivering my uncle's eulogy, his daughters handed me their written words to read. I structured it into a narrative and ensured that I could look up from time to time, making it feel more heartfelt and engaging.

6. Project Your Voice

Whether speaking in a small chapel or a large hall, ensure your voice reaches the audience. If a microphone is available, use it, but don't be afraid to adjust your volume as needed.

7. Let Emotion Show, But Maintain Composure

A eulogy is an emotional speech, and it is okay to show emotion. However, if tears start to take over, pause for a moment, take a breath, and continue at your own pace.

Handling Emotions While Speaking

Delivering a eulogy can be one of the most emotionally challenging moments of your life. Even if you feel fully prepared, emotions can surface unexpectedly. Here are ways to stay composed:

- **Accept That Emotions Are Natural** – Do not feel pressured to hold back tears or appear completely composed. A eulogy is a personal and emotional moment, and showing emotion is a sign of deep love and connection.
- **Pause When Needed** – If you feel overwhelmed, take a moment to collect yourself. The audience will understand.

- **Find a Focal Point** – Looking at a supportive face in the audience or focusing on a comforting visual (such as a framed photo of the deceased) can provide reassurance.

- **Have a Support Person Nearby** – If you are concerned about becoming too emotional, ask a trusted friend or family member to stand by you for moral support or take over if necessary.

- **Use a Handwritten Note with Personal Encouragement** – Writing a small message at the top of your notes, such as "Take your time" or "Breathe," can serve as a comforting reminder.

- **Keep a Glass of Water Close** – Taking a sip can provide a natural pause and help regain composure if your throat tightens with emotion.

During my father's eulogy, there were moments when I had to stop and take a breath. I found that pausing and looking just above the congregation, rather than directly at grieving faces, helped me regain my composure and continue.

Delivering a eulogy is an act of love and remembrance. While it may feel overwhelming, remember that the audience is there to support you, not judge you. Speak from the heart, embrace the emotions that arise, and trust that your words will honour your loved one in the most meaningful way possible.

With preparation, deep breaths, and the courage to speak from the heart, you will find the strength to deliver a eulogy that pays tribute to the life, love, and legacy of the person you are remembering.

Part 3: Heartfelt Eulogy Examples by Age

FOR NEWBORN AND INFANTS (0– 1 YEAR OLD)

1. Cradled in Heaven's Light

Opening: "We are gathered here today with hearts that are heavy with sorrow yet filled with immense love for [Name]. Though [his/her] time with us was brief, the love [he/she] brought into this world was limitless. We may not understand why God called [Name] home so soon, but we take comfort in knowing that [he/she] is now cradled in Heaven's eternal light."

Middle: "From the moment [Name] arrived, [he/she] filled our hearts with joy. Though [his/her] days were few, every second was a testament to love. [Insert a personal story about a moment with Name, such as holding their tiny hands, watching them sleep peacefully, or the way they responded to a loved one's voice.] These moments, though brief, will remain etched in our hearts forever."

"Even in sorrow, we give thanks for the time we had with [Name]. [He/She] reminded us of the miracle of life and the purity of love. Though [he/she] was with us for only a short time, [his/her] presence changed us in ways we never expected."

"[Name] was a precious soul, a gift from God, entrusted to us for a fleeting moment. We grieve not only the time we lost but also the laughter and love that would have filled [his/her] days."

Closing: "Though our arms are empty, our hearts are full of the love we will always have for [Name]. We trust in God's promise that one day we will be reunited in His Kingdom, where sorrow is no more, and love is everlasting."

2. A Love That Knows No End

Opening: "Today, we come together to honour the short yet profoundly meaningful life of [Name]. Though [he/she] was with us for only a little while, [his/her] presence changed us forever. We grieve today, not because love has ended, but because it continues on, yearning for a child who has already found peace in Heaven."

Middle: "[Name] never spoke a word, yet [his/her] life spoke volumes about love, hope, and the beauty of existence. [Insert personal story about how Name's presence brought hope and joy.] The love [Name] brought into this world is everlasting, and we take comfort in knowing that [his/her] soul is wrapped in divine grace."

"The joy of expecting [Name] filled our hearts with dreams and hopes. Though [he/she] did not get to grow into those dreams, [his/her] spirit remains with us, guiding us in love and remembrance."

"There is no footprint too small to leave an imprint on this world, and [Name] left a profound impact on everyone who loved [him/her]."

Closing: "As we say goodbye today, we do so with faith that God has welcomed [Name] into His loving embrace. Until we meet again, may we find peace in the love we shared."

3. Safe in God's Arms

Opening: "Though our hearts are burdened with grief today, we find solace in knowing that [Name] is safe in the arms of our Lord. [He/She] came into our lives like a gentle whisper, filling our hearts with joy and love that will never fade."

Middle: "[Name]'s life, though brief, was filled with love beyond measure. [Insert personal moment - perhaps a tender lullaby sung at night, the warmth of tiny hands, or the joy of simply holding them close.] Though [he/she] did not have the chance to experience the fullness of life on Earth, [he/she] knew only love and warmth."

"Each heartbeat, each tiny movement, each precious moment was a blessing that will remain with us forever."

"We take comfort in knowing that [Name] is surrounded by angels, embraced in love, and watching over us."

Closing: "We release [Name] into God's care, trusting in His divine love. Though we part today, we will always hold [Name] in our hearts."

4. A Soul Too Pure for This World

Opening: "Some souls are simply too pure for this world, and [Name] was one of them. Though our time together was short, the love [he/she] brought into our lives was infinite."

Middle: "From the moment [Name] was born, [he/she] radiated a peace that filled our hearts. [Insert a personal memory - perhaps a moment of quiet bonding, a whispered prayer, or a smile shared in the soft morning light.]"

"Though we wish we had more time, we are grateful for the gift of knowing and loving [Name]."

"We trust that God, in His wisdom, has welcomed [Name] into His kingdom, where there is no pain, no sorrow, only everlasting joy."

Closing: "As we say goodbye, we do so with gratitude for the time we had. [Name] is not truly gone, for love does not end - it simply takes on new form. Until we meet again, may [he/she] rest in eternal peace."

FOR YOUNG CHILDREN (AGES 1-6)

1. A Spirit Too Bright for This World

Opening: "It is with broken hearts that we gather today to celebrate the life of [Name], a child whose joy, curiosity, and innocence brightened the lives of all who knew [him/her]. Though [his/her] time on Earth was short, the love [he/she] gave and received will remain with us forever."

Middle: "[Name] was a child full of life and wonder. [Insert a story about Name's favourite things - perhaps their love for bedtime stories, laughter that filled the room, or the way they clung tightly to their loved ones.] [His/Her] joy was infectious, and [his/her] presence a gift to everyone around."

"Each day with [Name] was a treasure, filled with laughter and endless curiosity about the world. [He/She] loved to explore, whether it was chasing butterflies in the backyard, building castles from blocks, or creating imaginary adventures. [Insert an example of a favourite activity or hobby they enjoyed most.]"

"We hold on to the beautiful memories of [Name], cherishing the love [he/she] shared and the lessons [he/she] unknowingly taught us. [Share a meaningful memory, such as a kind act Name did for a friend or family member, a phrase they loved to say, or a moment that perfectly captured their unique personality.]"

Closing: "Though we must let [Name] go, we do so knowing that [his/her] light continues to shine in Heaven. We carry [his/her] spirit within us, and we trust in the Lord's promise that we will be reunited one day."

2. The Joy of [Name]'s Presence

Opening: "It is said that children are God's greatest blessing, and [Name] was indeed a gift to all who knew [him/her]. We gather not only in sorrow but in gratitude for the joy [Name] brought to our lives."

Middle: "[Name] lived with a heart full of love, kindness, and laughter. [Insert personal memory - perhaps how Name loved playing outside, had a favourite song, or always reached for a hug.] Every moment with [Name] was precious, a reminder of life's purest joys."

"[Name] had a way of lighting up a room, bringing smiles to those around [him/her]. [He/She] reminded us all of the beauty in laughter and the purity of childhood. Whether it was through a silly joke, a playful dance, or a loving hug, [Name] had a unique way of making people feel loved. [Include a specific example of a funny or heartwarming moment that embodies their joyful spirit.]"

"Even though [Name] is no longer with us physically, [his/her] laughter, love, and joy will live on in our hearts forever. [Share a comforting memory - perhaps a bedtime routine, a phrase they always said, or a special bond they had with a family member.]"

Closing: "As we say farewell, let us remember the words of Isaiah 41:10, 'Do not fear, for I am with you; do not be dismayed, for I am your God.' May this promise bring us peace, knowing that [Name] is safe in the arms of our Heavenly Father."

3. A Love That Lives Beyond Time

Opening: "To love a child is to know the deepest kind of love, and today, as we say farewell to [Name], we hold onto that love more fiercely than ever."

Middle: "[Name] was full of energy, kindness, and curiosity. [Insert story about their favourite hobbies, dreams for the future, or moments of laughter and adventure.] [He/She] taught us to find joy in the smallest things, to embrace life with open arms."

"Though our time with [Name] was shorter than we ever imagined, every moment was a gift. [Reflect on a time they made a difference in the life of someone close, whether it was through a kind gesture, an unexpected hug, or a simple but profound expression of love.]"

"We trust that the same God who gave us the gift of [Name] now holds [him/her] close. In that trust, we find the courage to carry on, knowing that love does not end - it only changes form. [Include a heartfelt recollection - perhaps a moment when their personality shone brightest, or a unique habit or trait that made them special.]"

Closing: "We entrust [Name] to God's care, knowing that [he/she] watches over us from above. Though [his/her] absence is deeply felt, [his/her] spirit will forever remain a part of us."

4. A Child's Heart, A Family's Love

Opening: "There are no words that can truly capture the pain of losing a child, and yet, there are no words more powerful than love. Today, we gather to celebrate the life of [Name], a child whose love and laughter will never be forgotten."

Middle: "[Name] was a source of boundless joy, full of curiosity and wonder. [Insert memory about their kindness, their favourite games, or how they brought people together.] [He/She] filled every moment with love, reminding us of the simple yet profound joys of life."

"Though we wish we had more time, we cherish the days we did have, knowing that [Name] was a blessing beyond words. [Include a moment when their kindness or playful nature shone through - perhaps a time they comforted a sibling, shared something special, or said something that warmed your heart.]"

"The loss of [Name] is immeasurable, but so is the love [he/she] left behind. That love will guide us, comfort us, and remain a part of our lives forever. [Share one final memory that brings peace, such as a bedtime prayer they loved, a favourite lullaby, or a family tradition they cherished.]"

Closing: "As we say goodbye, we find solace in knowing that [Name] is embraced in God's eternal love. May [he/she] rest in peace, and may we carry [his/her] light forward in our hearts."

FOR CHILDREN (AGES 7-12)

1. A Life Full of Promise

Opening: "We come together today to celebrate the life of [Name], a bright and beautiful soul who touched our lives in immeasurable ways. Though [his/her] time with us was far too short, the joy, love, and laughter [he/she] brought will remain forever in our hearts."

Middle: "[Name] had a spirit that shone so brightly. [Insert a personal memory about their curiosity, enthusiasm for life, or a moment when they amazed those around them with their kindness or intelligence.] Whether [he/she] was exploring new adventures, creating something wonderful, or sharing laughter with friends and family, [Name] left an undeniable mark on this world."

"[Name] had dreams as big as the sky. [Include a story about what they wanted to be when they grew up, a favourite hobby, or how they spent their time pursuing things that made them happy.] It's in those dreams that we see the light of [his/her] spirit still shining."

"One of the most beautiful things about [Name] was [his/her] kindness. [He/She] had a heart full of love, always looking out for others and making sure no one felt left out. [Share a moment when they showed incredible kindness to a friend, sibling, or even a stranger.]"

Closing: "Though we wish we had more time; we are grateful for every moment we shared with [Name]. We take comfort in knowing that [he/she] is now in the loving embrace of our Heavenly Father, watching over us. We will carry [his/her] spirit in our hearts, cherishing the love, the laughter, and the lessons [he/she] gave us."

2. A Heart as Big as the World

Opening: "Today, we gather to remember [Name], a child whose love knew no bounds. [He/She] was a light in the lives of so many, always ready with a smile, a kind word, or a helping hand."

Middle: "[Name] had an incredible way of making people feel special. [Insert a memory of how they made someone laugh, encouraged a friend, or brightened a difficult day.] [His/Her] generosity and warmth touched everyone who knew [him/her]."

"It was the little things that made [Name] so special. [Include a story about a unique habit or favourite saying that brought joy to those around them.]"

"[Name] was always full of energy, eager to explore, play, and learn. Whether [he/she] was riding a bike through the neighbourhood, drawing masterpieces with crayons, or collecting treasures from nature, [his/her] joy for life was infectious. [Add a memory of their favourite pastime or an adventure they loved to embark on.]"

Closing: "Though our hearts ache with sorrow, we find comfort in knowing that [Name] is now in the arms of God, free from pain, and surrounded by love. We will carry [his/her] kindness and laughter with us always, honouring [his/her] legacy by sharing that same love with the world."

3. A Young Life, A Lasting Legacy

Opening: "We never imagined we would have to say goodbye to [Name] so soon, but today we gather not just in grief, but in celebration of the incredible life [he/she] lived. Though [his/her] years were far too few, [he/she] made a profound impact on those around [him/her]."

Middle: "From an early age, [Name] had a gift for making people smile. [Insert an anecdote about their sense of humour, infectious laugh, or ability to bring joy to others.] Whether it was a silly joke, a dance in the rain, or a simple act of love, [he/she] had a way of making the world brighter."

"[Name] had a deep love for [insert favourite activity - whether sports, music, reading, or another passion]. [He/She] approached everything with excitement and dedication, always striving to do [his/her] best. [Share a moment when they achieved something they were proud of or worked hard toward a goal.]"

"One of the most remarkable things about [Name] was [his/her] ability to bring people together. [He/She] had a way of making everyone feel included, valued, and loved. [Insert a story of a time they helped a friend, comforted someone in need, or made a difference with their kindness.]"

Closing: "Though our hearts grieve, we find hope in knowing that [Name] is at peace. We will hold onto the love [he/she] gave us and honour [his/her] memory by carrying that love forward. May we find strength in faith and comfort in knowing that one day, we will be reunited."

4. A Life That Taught Us Love

Opening: "[Name] may have had a short time on this Earth, but [he/she] filled every moment with love, laughter, and light. We gather here today to remember a child whose heart was pure and whose spirit was a gift to us all."

Middle: "[Name] loved deeply and was deeply loved. [Insert a memory about a moment of affection, a special bond with a family member, or a time when their love was evident.]"

"[Name] had a special way of looking at the world - full of wonder, excitement, and joy. [He/She] saw adventure in the smallest things, whether it was chasing fireflies on a summer night, building forts from blankets, or dreaming of what [he/she] would be one day. [Include a story about something they were passionate about or a dream they shared.]"

"Perhaps the greatest lesson [Name] taught us was how to love without hesitation. [He/She] gave love freely, shared happiness generously, and lived each day with an open heart. [Insert a story of a time they comforted someone, showed kindness, or made a selfless gesture.]"

Closing: "Though we wish we had more time, we are forever grateful for the gift of [Name]. We know that [he/she] is safe in the loving arms of God, and we will carry [his/her] love in our hearts forever. May we honour [his/her] memory by continuing to love as [he/she] did, without fear and without limits."

Chapter 9

FOR TEENS AND YOUNG ADULTS (AGES 13-21)

The loss of a young person is a tragedy that no words can fully ease. Whether due to unexpected circumstances or illness, losing someone so full of life, dreams, and aspirations leaves an indescribable void. Though we grieve deeply, we also come together to honour the joy, passion, and love they brought into the world. These eulogies offer heartfelt tributes, allowing those who knew and loved them to find comfort in their memory, in faith, and in the knowledge that their spirit lives on.

1. A Life Full of Promise

Opening: "Today, we gather with hearts heavy with grief, yet filled with love, to honour the life of [Name]. A life so full of promise, dreams, and endless possibilities, yet one taken from us far too soon. Though our sorrow is deep, we find comfort in remembering the incredible person [Name] was and the impact [he/she] had on all of us."

Middle: "[Name] had a spirit that could light up any room. [Insert a memory of their enthusiasm for life - whether excelling in school, their love for sports, music, or the kindness they showed to those around them.] [He/She] had an incredible way of making people feel seen, understood, and valued."

"[Name] was never afraid to dream. [Share a memory about something they were passionate about - a future career goal, a project they were working on, or a talent they pursued with determination.] Though we grieve today, we also celebrate the drive and ambition [he/she] carried, inspiring us all."

"Perhaps most remarkable was [Name]'s kindness. [Insert a story about how they helped a friend, comforted a sibling, or stood up for someone in need.] These acts of love and generosity will forever be a part of [his/her] legacy."

Closing: "Though [Name]'s journey was shorter than we ever imagined, [he/she] left a lasting imprint on our hearts. We take solace in knowing that [he/she] is now embraced by the love of our Heavenly Father, free from pain, watching over us. We will carry [his/her] love, laughter, and spirit with us always."

2. Gone Too Soon, But Never Forgotten

Opening: "The world feels dimmer without [Name] here. There are no words to truly capture the depth of our sorrow, and yet, there is so much to say about the light [he/she] brought into our lives. Today, we grieve, but we also remember - a life filled with love, adventure, and the unwavering energy of youth."

Middle: "[Name] lived every day with a fearless heart. [Insert a memory about their adventurous nature, a time they made you laugh, or a passion they pursued without hesitation.] [He/She] taught us that life is meant to be lived to the fullest, that laughter should never be held back, and that love should be given freely."

"Even in times of struggle, [Name] faced challenges with resilience and grace. [Share a story about how they overcame hardship, helped someone in need, or found joy even in difficult moments.] These are the qualities we will forever cherish."

"One of [Name]'s greatest gifts was the way [he/she] made people feel. [He/She] had a way of uplifting others, offering a shoulder to lean on, or simply making someone's day brighter. [Include a moment when their presence changed someone's life for the better.]"

Closing: "As we say our goodbyes, we do so knowing that [Name]'s love, joy, and spirit will never fade. Though [his/her] time here was brief, [he/she] lived a life that touched so many. May we honour [him/her] by carrying forward the love and light [he/she] brought into this world."

3. A Legacy of Love and Strength

Opening: "Today, we remember [Name], a young soul whose kindness, ambition, and love for life were undeniable. While the pain of losing [him/her] is immense, we find strength in the memories shared, the lives [he/she] touched, and the love that will remain with us forever."

Middle: "[Name] was a force of nature. [Insert a memory about their dedication to a goal, the way they embraced challenges, or how they inspired those around them.] [He/She] tackled life with passion, always striving to make a difference."

"One of the greatest joys of knowing [Name] was experiencing [his/her] unwavering love for family and friends. [Share a moment where they showed deep care for a loved one or went out of their way to help others.]"

"Even though [Name] is no longer with us physically, [his/her] legacy lives on in the lessons [he/she] left behind. [Include an example of something they taught you - whether resilience, compassion, or how to find joy in the little things.]"

Closing: "Though our hearts ache, we take comfort in knowing that [Name] is at peace, watching over us with love. We will continue to honour [his/her] memory by living with the same passion, kindness, and strength that [he/she] showed us every day."

4. Forever in Our Hearts

Opening: "There are people who, even in a short time, leave an impact so great that they change the world around them. [Name] was one of those people. Today, we mourn, but we also celebrate a life that was deeply loved and a spirit that will never be forgotten."

Middle: "[Name] had an infectious enthusiasm for life. [Insert a story of their adventures - perhaps traveling, achieving a milestone, or how they embraced life's opportunities with excitement.] [He/She] taught us that life is meant to be embraced with an open heart and an adventurous spirit."

"But more than anything, [Name]'s greatest gift was love. [He/She] gave love without hesitation, whether through a kind word, a thoughtful gesture, or the simple act of being there. [Share an example of a time they supported someone through hardship, made a family member proud, or showed compassion beyond measure.]"

"Even in sorrow, we find gratitude for having known [Name]. The memories we shared, the laughter, and the love will be with us forever. [Include a specific farewell message - perhaps a phrase they always said or a promise to honour their memory.]"

Closing: "Though [Name]'s physical presence is no longer here, their spirit remains woven into our lives. We honour [him/her] by carrying forward the love [he/she] shared, by living with courage and kindness, and by never forgetting the joy [he/she] brought to this world."

5. A Soul Wise Beyond Their Years

Opening: "Some people, no matter how young, seem to possess wisdom beyond their years. [Name] was one of those souls. Today, as we gather in sorrow, we also remember the wisdom, kindness, and strength that [he/she] showed throughout [his/her] life."

Middle: "[Name] always had an old soul. [Insert an anecdote about their thoughtful advice, their ability to comfort others, or a time they displayed a level of maturity beyond their years.] [He/She] had a way of understanding people in a way that was rare and beautiful."

"One of [his/her] greatest qualities was the way [he/she] looked out for others. [Include a story about how they went out of their way to help a friend, stood up for what was right, or made someone feel valued and loved.]"

"Even though [Name]'s journey was cut short, the impact [he/she] left behind is immeasurable. [Share a time when they taught you something - whether it was through their actions, their resilience, or the simple way they approached life with open-heartedness.]"

Closing: "While we wish we had more time, we are grateful for the time we did have with [Name]. We find comfort in knowing that [he/she] now rests in eternal peace, forever watching over us."

6. A Friend to All, A Light to Many

Opening: "To know [Name] was to know true friendship, laughter, and joy. [He/She] had a way of making everyone feel included, of turning strangers into friends and bringing happiness wherever [he/she] went. Today, as we grieve, we also remember and celebrate the love [he/she] shared with us all."

Middle: "[Name] had a rare gift for making people smile. [Insert a story about their humour, a time they lifted someone's spirits, or a prank or joke that still makes you laugh today.] Even in the hardest moments, [he/she] found a way to bring joy."

"But more than just laughter, [Name] had a heart that was open and kind. [Share an example of how they helped someone through a tough time, made sure no one felt left out, or went above and beyond to make others feel special.]"

"Though [Name] is no longer physically with us, [he/she] will always be present in the memories we cherish, in the love [he/she] shared, and in the way [he/she] brought people together."

Closing: "It is difficult to say goodbye to someone who was so full of life, love, and laughter. But as we honour [Name] today, we promise to carry [his/her] light forward - to be kinder, to laugh more, and to embrace life as fully as [he/she] did."

Chapter 10

FOR SPOUSES AND PARTNERS

1. Remembering a Life Partner

Opening: "Today, I stand before you not just with grief, but with gratitude for the incredible gift that was [Name]. [He/She] was not just my spouse, but my best friend, my confidant, and my greatest love. Though my heart is heavy, I find solace in knowing that [he/she] lived a life full of love, laughter, and purpose."

Middle: "From the moment we met, [Name] changed my life in ways I could never have imagined. [Insert a personal memory about how you met, a special moment in your relationship, or what made your love story unique.]"

"Our days were filled with love, with laughter, and with challenges that we faced together. [Share a moment that showcases their strength, kindness, or unwavering devotion.]"

"Even in the hardest times, [Name] had a way of bringing light to every situation. [Describe a humorous or heartfelt moment that demonstrates their personality.]"

Closing: "Though I will miss [Name] every single day, I take comfort in knowing that love never truly dies. I will carry [his/her] love with me in my heart and honour [his/her] memory by living the way [he/she] would have wanted - full of kindness, laughter, and love."

2. Finding Strength in Love and Memories

Opening: "It is difficult to find the words to say goodbye to someone who was my heart, my home, and my everything. [Name] was more than my spouse - [he/she] was my partner in every sense of the word. Today, we gather to remember [his/her] beautiful soul and the love that continues to live on."

Middle: "[Name] and I built a life together - one full of adventure, laughter, and unwavering support. [Share a story about a journey you took together, an inside joke, or a habit that brought joy to your relationship.]"

"[He/She] had a way of making every day special, even in the smallest ways. [Insert a memory about how they showed love daily - whether through a morning routine, a favourite phrase, or a simple act of kindness.]"

"I will forever cherish the life we built together, the dreams we shared, and the love that will never fade. [Mention a lesson they taught you, or a way they shaped who you are today.]"

Closing: "Though my heart aches with loss, I find strength in the love we shared. [Name] may no longer be by my side, but [his/her] love surrounds me every day. I will honour [his/her] legacy by continuing to live fully, just as [he/she] would have wanted."

3. Honouring a Marriage and Shared Life

Opening: "Marriage is a journey - one of love, commitment, and unwavering support. Today, I stand here to honour my partner, my love, my best friend, [Name]. [He/She] was my home, my rock, and the person who knew me better than anyone else."

Middle: "From the moment we said 'I do,' we built a life together, hand in hand. [Share a wedding memory, a milestone anniversary, or a cherished tradition.]"

"No marriage is without challenges, but what made ours so special was how we faced them together. [Include a moment when your spouse showed resilience, forgiveness, or unwavering support.]"

"Even in the quietest moments, [Name] had a way of making me feel loved. [Describe a simple, everyday gesture that you will miss the most - holding hands, the way they looked at you, a nickname they had for you.]"

Closing: "Though [Name] is no longer physically with me, I know that our love is eternal. I will continue to carry [his/her] love with me in every step I take, in every choice I make, and in every memory that I hold dear."

4. The Light of My Life

Opening: "There are few people in this world who can light up a room simply by being in it. [Name] was one of those people. My life was richer, fuller, and more beautiful because of [him/her], and today, as I say goodbye, I also celebrate the love and happiness [he/she] brought to my world."

Middle: "[Name] had an incredible way of making ordinary days extraordinary. [Share a memory of a simple, everyday moment that captures their personality - a way they made you laugh, a habit they had that was uniquely them.]"

"[He/She] always believed in me, even when I doubted myself. [Describe a time when they lifted you up, encouraged you, or helped you become the best version of yourself.]"

"Our love story may not have lasted forever in time, but it will last forever in my heart. [Reflect on a promise you made to each other, or a sentiment they always expressed that you will carry forward.]"

Closing: "Though today is filled with sorrow, I choose to remember the love and light that [Name] brought into my life. I am a better person because of [him/her], and I will continue to honour [his/her] love in everything I do."

5. Until We Meet Again

Opening: "Saying goodbye to [Name] feels impossible. [He/She] was the love of my life, my greatest joy, and my truest friend. Though my heart is broken, I take comfort in knowing that love never truly fades."

Middle: "Our life together was filled with moments big and small that I will cherish forever. [Share a special memory, such as a trip, a surprise they planned, or a quiet moment that defined your love.]"

"[Name] had a way of making every day feel special. [Include a story about their kindness, a simple daily ritual you shared, or a phrase they often said that still brings you comfort.]"

"Though I will miss [his/her] voice, laughter, and presence, I know that [he/she] is still with me in spirit. [Describe a way you will carry their memory forward - whether through honouring a shared dream, continuing a tradition, or embracing the love they gave.]"

Closing: "While today we say farewell, I know that one day, we will be together again. Until then, I will hold onto our love, our memories, and the faith that sustains me. Rest in peace, my love."

6. My Rock, My Refuge

Opening: "[Name] was more than my spouse - [he/she] was my safe haven, my strength in times of trouble, and my greatest love. The world feels quieter now without [him/her], but the love we shared continues to echo in my heart."

Middle: "Through every storm, [Name] stood by my side, always offering a steady hand and a loving heart. [Share a memory of how they comforted you in difficult times, provided wisdom, or helped you find your way.]"

"Even in the simplest moments - morning coffee, evening walks, quiet conversations - [Name] made life meaningful. [Describe a special tradition or ritual that defined your relationship.]"

"The greatest gift [he/she] gave me was unwavering love. [Reflect on how they shaped your life and left a legacy that will always remain.]"

Closing: "Though I must walk forward without [Name], I know I am not truly alone. Love never ends, and I will cherish [his/her] presence in my heart forever."

7. A Love That Knew No Bounds

Opening: "Love is the thread that connects us beyond this life, and the love [Name] and I shared will never fade. Though [his/her] physical presence is gone, the love remains, eternal and unbreakable."

Middle: "[Name] taught me what it means to love unconditionally. [Share an example of their selflessness, generosity, or the way they cared for family and friends.]"

"Every day with [Name] was a blessing, filled with laughter, adventure, and joy. [Describe a memory of their humour, spirit, or how they made even ordinary days special.]"

"Though I grieve deeply, I also give thanks for the time we had together. [Mention something they always said, a belief they held, or a lesson they taught you that you carry forward.]"

Closing: "[Name] was my heart, my home, my everything. Though I long for one more moment, I take comfort in knowing that love is eternal and we will be reunited once more."

8. A Life Well-Lived, A Love Well Shared

Opening: "A great love is not measured by years but by the depth of devotion shared. [Name] and I lived a life filled with love, and though [he/she] is no longer with me, that love will never diminish."

Middle: "[Name] was the kind of person who made life brighter for everyone. [Share a story of how they lifted others up, inspired those around them, or always found joy in the little things.]"

"We built a life together - a beautiful tapestry of memories, challenges, and triumphs. [Describe a meaningful moment in your relationship that defined your bond.]"

"Though I ache for one more day, I know [Name] would want me to continue forward with strength, carrying our love into each new day."

Closing: "While today we say goodbye, I know this is not the end. Love is not bound by time, and [Name] will forever be a part of me. Until we meet again, I will honour [his/her] memory by living with the love and grace [he/she] always showed."

Chapter 11

FOR PARENTS AND GRANDPARENTS

1. A Father's Strength and Love

Opening: "Today, we gather to celebrate the life of a man who was not just my father but my hero. [Name] was the foundation of our family, a source of strength, wisdom, and unwavering love. His legacy is one of kindness, resilience, and faith."

Middle: "From the earliest days of my life, my father taught me what it means to work hard, love deeply, and stand firm in my beliefs. [Share a personal story of his guidance, a lesson he taught, or a moment that defined his strength.]"

"He was always there - whether it was cheering me on from the sidelines, offering quiet words of wisdom, or simply being present when I needed him most. [Insert a memory that captures his unwavering support.]"

"Even in his hardest moments, he led with grace and dignity. [Reflect on how he faced challenges and the example he set.]"

Closing: "Though my father is no longer physically with us, his love and wisdom will continue to guide me. I will honour him by living as he did - with courage, compassion, and integrity."

2. A Mother's Gentle and Enduring Love

Opening: "There are few forces in this world as powerful as a mother's love. Today, as we remember [Name], we celebrate the warmth, strength, and kindness she gave so freely to all who knew her."

Middle: "She was the heart of our home, the one who made even ordinary days feel special. [Share a memory of her love, whether through her cooking, the stories she told, or the way she made everyone feel safe.]"

"Her love was unwavering. She was there through every joy and every hardship, always reminding us that no matter what, we were never alone. [Insert a story about her unconditional support.]"

"She taught us what it means to be strong, not just in times of ease, but in times of trial. [Describe a moment when she showed resilience and inspired those around her.]"

Closing: "Though she is no longer with us, her love will never fade. It lives on in the lessons she taught, the kindness she showed, and the family she nurtured."

3. A Grandfather's Wisdom and Guidance

Opening: "A grandfather is both a storyteller and a teacher, a source of wisdom and warmth. Today, we celebrate the life of [Name], a man whose legacy will live on in the countless lives he touched."

Middle: "He had a way of making every moment meaningful, whether it was through his stories, his laughter, or his quiet strength. [Share a cherished memory that highlights his wisdom or humour.]"

"His presence was a constant source of comfort and encouragement. [Describe how he inspired or mentored you or others.]"

"Even in his later years, his love for family never wavered. He made sure we knew we were cherished. [Include a moment that reflects his devotion to his family.]"

Closing: "Though we grieve his loss, we are grateful for the lessons he passed on and the love he left behind. We will honour him by living with the same grace and wisdom he exemplified."

4. A Grandmother's Love and Legacy

Opening: "Grandmothers have a way of making the world feel a little softer, a little kinder, and a lot more filled with love. [Name] was a pillar of warmth, grace, and generosity, and today, we honour her life and legacy."

Middle: "She was a storyteller, a nurturer, and the heart of our family. [Share a favourite story, tradition, or lesson she passed down.]"

"Her wisdom was gentle but powerful. [Reflect on advice she gave or a moment she guided you through.]"

"Through her kindness, she left an imprint on every person she met. [Describe how she made people feel loved and valued.]"

Closing: "Though she is no longer with us, her legacy of love continues. We will carry her spirit forward, sharing the kindness and warmth she so effortlessly gave."

5. A Father's Legacy of Strength and Kindness

Opening: "A father is a guiding light, a steady hand, and a source of unwavering love. Today, we honour the life of [Name], a man whose strength, kindness, and wisdom shaped the lives of everyone around him."

Middle: "[Name] was a man of integrity, always leading by example. [Share a moment that reflects his character - his work ethic, his generosity, or his role as a protector.]"

"He found joy in the simple things - family dinners, long walks, or teaching us life's lessons. [Include a personal story that captures these quiet, meaningful moments.]"

"His love was never loud, but it was always present. In the way he supported us, encouraged us, and made sure we knew we were cherished. [Describe a time he showed his love in an understated but powerful way.]"

Closing: "Though he is no longer physically with us, his love and teachings will forever be our foundation. We will carry his strength forward, honouring him with the way we live our lives."

6. A Mother's Gentle Strength

Opening: "Mothers have a way of making everything feel safe and warm, and [Name] was no exception. She was the heart of our family, filling our lives with love, wisdom, and grace."

Middle: "She taught us what it means to love unconditionally. [Share a story that reflects her nurturing nature, whether through her comforting words, her selfless actions, or the way she always put family first.]"

"No matter how difficult life became, she carried herself with dignity and strength. [Describe a time when she faced adversity with courage and faith.]"

"Her presence was a gift, and her laughter, kindness, and unwavering love will be missed deeply. [Include a favourite memory that truly captures who she was.]"

Closing: "We will honour her by carrying her lessons forward - by loving as she loved, giving as she gave, and living with the same kindness she showed every day."

7. A Grandfather's Love and Lessons

Opening: "Grandfathers have a way of making us feel like the most important person in the world. Today, we celebrate the life of [Name], a man whose love and wisdom shaped generations."

Middle: "He had a story for every occasion, a lesson hidden in every conversation. [Share a memory of a piece of advice he gave, a skill he passed down, or a tradition he upheld.]"

"Whether it was through his quiet encouragement or his steady presence, he made a lasting impact. [Describe how he supported or mentored you or others.]"

"Even in his later years, he never stopped teaching, laughing, or showing love. [Reflect on a small but meaningful moment that captures his character.]"

Closing: "We are grateful for the time we had with him and the legacy of love and wisdom he leaves behind. His spirit will always be a part of us."

8. A Grandmother's Gentle Spirit

Opening: "To be loved by a grandmother is to be wrapped in warmth, kindness, and wisdom. [Name] was the heart of our family, and today, we honour the beautiful life she lived."

Middle: "She had a way of making everyone feel special. [Describe a memory that captures her warmth - whether it was baking cookies, reading bedtime stories, or simply holding your hand.]"

"Her wisdom was given freely, her love never wavered. [Include a story of advice she shared, a tradition she passed down, or a moment she provided comfort.]"

"She made our world a brighter place, one filled with laughter, faith, and unconditional love. [Share a small but powerful moment that truly represents her spirit.]"

Closing: "Though we say goodbye, her love will remain with us forever. We will honour her by carrying forward the kindness and faith she so effortlessly shared."

9. A Father Who Led with Love and Faith

Opening: "A father's love is a steady presence, a strong foundation, and a quiet reassurance that we are never alone. Today, we remember [Name], a man whose faith and love guided our lives."

Middle: "He led not just with words, but with actions - showing us what it means to live a life of faith and integrity. [Share a moment when he embodied these values.]"

"His love was evident in all he did, from the sacrifices he made for his family to the joy he found in simple, everyday moments. [Describe a memory of his devotion to family, his humour, or his unwavering belief in something greater.]"

"He taught us to trust in God, to love deeply, and to never take life's blessings for granted. [Reflect on how his faith shaped you and those around him.]"

Closing: "Though he is no longer with us, his legacy of faith and love will guide us always. We will honour him by living with the same strength and devotion he showed every day."

10. A Mother Who Was a Beacon of Love

Opening: "A mother's love is the first love we ever know, and it shapes us in ways we never fully realize until she is gone. [Name] was a mother like no other - a guiding light, a source of strength, and the heart of our family."

Middle: "She had a way of making every person she met feel special. [Describe a time she went out of her way to help someone, made someone smile, or simply showed kindness in a quiet way.]"

"Her love was not just in words, but in actions - in the meals she cooked, the prayers she said, and the way she always knew just what to say. [Share a memory that captures her selflessness and warmth.]"

"Even in the hardest moments, she remained our rock. Her faith never wavered, and her love never dimmed. [Reflect on her strength and the lessons she passed on.]"

Closing: "Though she is gone, her love will never leave us. We will honour her by living as she did - with grace, kindness, and unshakable faith."

Chapter 12

FOR SIBLINGS AND CLOSE FRIENDS

1. A Brother's Lifelong Bond

Opening: "Losing a brother is like losing a part of yourself. Today, we gather not just in sorrow, but in celebration of a life well lived - a life that was full of love, laughter, and unwavering support. [Name] was not just my brother, but my lifelong friend, my greatest ally, and my role model."

Alternative Opening: "A brother is more than just family - he is a protector, a friend, and a lifelong companion. [Name] was all of those things and more. While we grieve today, we also honour the countless memories and the deep connection we shared."

Middle: "From childhood adventures to the challenges of adulthood, [Name] was always there. [Share a memory of growing up together - playing games, supporting each other through tough times, or a funny story that captures his spirit.]"

"He had a way of making every moment count, whether it was through his humour, his kindness, or his determination. [Describe his character and how he impacted those around him.]"

"No matter what life threw our way, I always knew I could count on him. [Reflect on his role as a brother, his loyalty, and the way he supported others.]"

Closing: "Though he is gone, the bond we shared will never be broken. I will carry his love and his memory with me always, and I will strive to honour his life by living mine with the same strength and kindness he did."

Alternative Closing: "Goodbyes are not forever, and this is not the end. I find comfort in knowing that one day, we will meet again, and until then, his spirit will live on in every cherished memory."

2. A Sister's Unbreakable Love

Opening: "A sister is a built-in best friend, a confidante, and a piece of your heart that can never be replaced. Today, we honour the beautiful life of [Name], my sister and my greatest friend."

Alternative Opening: "Some bonds cannot be broken - not even by death. My sister, [Name], was one of the most important people in my life, and while she may no longer be here, her love and presence will always be felt."

Middle: "Growing up with [Name] meant never facing anything alone. [Share a childhood memory - whether it was late-night talks, inside jokes, or a time she stood up for you.]"

"She was my biggest cheerleader, my strongest supporter, and the person who knew me better than anyone. [Describe her personality - her kindness, strength, or the way she brought joy to others.]"

"Her love was a gift, and I will carry it with me always. [Reflect on the lessons she taught you, the strength she showed, and how she changed your life.]"

Closing: "Though she may be gone, her spirit remains in the love she gave, the memories she created, and the lives she touched. I will honour her by carrying forward the love she so freely shared."

Alternative Closing: "Sisters are forever, and so is love. Though we say goodbye today, I know she will always be with me, guiding me and loving me from beyond."

3. A Best Friend Like No Other

Opening: "Some friendships go beyond words - they become a part of who we are. [Name] was more than my best friend - [he/she] was my family, my partner in adventure, and the person I could always count on."

Alternative Opening: "True friendship is one of life's greatest gifts, and I was blessed beyond measure to have shared that gift with [Name]. Today, we honour the joy, laughter, and love [he/she] brought into our lives."

Middle: "From the moment we met, I knew [Name] was someone special. [Share how you became friends, a memorable adventure, or an inside joke you shared.]"

"Through the highs and lows of life, [Name] was always there. [Describe how they supported you, the way they lifted others up, and what made their friendship so unique.]"

"No matter what, I always knew I had a friend in [Name]. [Reflect on their loyalty, the lessons they taught you, and the impact they had on your life.]"

Closing: "Though life will never be the same without [Name], I will carry our friendship in my heart forever. The love of a true friend never fades."

Alternative Closing: "As I say goodbye, I do so with gratitude - for the time we had, the laughter we shared, and the love that will never leave me. Rest in peace, my dearest friend."

4. A Brother's Steadfast Presence

Opening: "A brother's love is a steady and unshakable force. Today, we gather to celebrate [Name], a man whose loyalty, kindness, and laughter filled our lives. He was more than just my brother - he was my greatest companion in this journey of life."

Alternative Opening: "Brothers share an unspoken bond - a connection that withstands the trials of time and distance. [Name] was my anchor, my friend, and someone I could always count on."

Middle: "From childhood mischief to adult challenges, we walked side by side. [Share a story of growing up together, a moment of support, or a memory that defines his character.]"

"His laughter was contagious, his presence reassuring, and his heart immeasurable. [Reflect on a time he brightened a dark day or made life's journey easier.]"

"Through every up and down, [Name] remained a constant source of strength and love. [Describe his generosity, protective nature, or the wisdom he imparted.]"

Closing: "Though the world feels emptier without him, I know his love and legacy will endure. I will live in a way that honours the lessons he taught me and the kindness he always shared."

Alternative Closing: "Goodbye for now, dear brother. One day, we will laugh together again. Until then, I will hold on to every memory and every moment of love we shared."

5. A Sister's Guiding Light

Opening: "A sister's love is woven into the fabric of our lives, a thread that never frays. Today, we honour [Name], a woman whose light, warmth, and love will never fade."

Alternative Opening: "To have a sister is to have a best friend for life. [Name] was that and so much more. She was my inspiration, my safe space, and my greatest supporter."

Middle: "She had a way of turning ordinary moments into lifelong memories. [Share a story about her playful spirit, her acts of kindness, or the wisdom she shared.]"

"[Name] always knew what to say, how to listen, and how to remind me that I was never alone. [Reflect on her compassion, loyalty, or the love she poured into every relationship.]"

"Even in her hardest days, she showed resilience and grace. [Describe a time she persevered, gave strength to others, or lived with courage.]"

Closing: "While my heart aches at her absence, I will carry her love with me always. She may be gone from sight, but never from my heart."

Alternative Closing: "Sisters are forever, and that is something even death cannot change. I will live with her love in my heart, knowing we will meet again."

6. A Best Friend Who Became Family

Opening: "Not all family is tied by blood. Some are bonded through love, loyalty, and time. [Name] was my best friend, my greatest confidant, and the person who made life richer just by being in it."

Alternative Opening: "Some friendships go beyond words - they become a part of who we are. [Name] was more than my best friend - [he/she] was my family, my partner in adventure, and the person I could always count on."

Middle: "We met as strangers and became inseparable. [Share a memory of how you met, an inside joke, or an experience that defined your friendship.]"

"[Name] had a way of making life brighter, of reminding me what truly mattered. [Reflect on a lesson they taught you or a way they lifted your spirit.]"

"Even in the hardest moments, [Name] stood by my side. [Describe how they supported you, and how they left a lasting impact on your life.]"

Closing: "Though life will never be the same without [Name], I will carry our friendship in my heart forever. The love of a true friend never fades."

Alternative Closing: "As I say goodbye, I do so with gratitude - for the time we had, the laughter we shared, and the love that will never leave me. Rest in peace, my dearest friend."

7. A Loyal and Trusted Companion

Opening: "True friendship is a rare and precious gift. [Name] was more than just a friend - [he/she] was a soul who understood me in a way no one else could."

Alternative Opening: "Some friendships define our lives, shaping who we are and who we become. [Name] was one of those friends - a light in my life that will never fade."

Middle: "[Name] had a way of always knowing what to say, how to lift my spirits, and how to turn an ordinary day into something memorable. [Share a special memory or habit that made them unique.]"

"No matter how much time passed or how far apart we were, we always picked up right where we left off. [Describe their loyalty, presence, and impact on your life.]"

"They were my confidant, my laughter, my second family. [Name] was someone I knew I could always count on."

Closing: "Though I grieve today, I find solace in knowing that the love and friendship we shared will never truly end."

Alternative Closing: "This is not goodbye, dear friend. This is simply, 'Until we meet again.'"

8. A Childhood Friend Who Was Always There

Opening: "Some friends are with us for a season, and some are with us for a lifetime. [Name] was the latter - a friend who stood beside me through every joy and every challenge."

Alternative Opening: "From childhood games to adulthood struggles, [Name] was my unwavering friend. Today, I honour the gift of their friendship."

Middle: "We grew up together, laughed together, and faced the world together. [Share a childhood story that reflects their presence in your life.]"

"Even as we grew older, [Name] remained constant - always offering support, laughter, and wisdom. [Describe a moment they made a difference in your life.]"

"They were more than a friend; they were a part of my heart."

Closing: "Though [Name] is gone, I will carry their love with me always, in every memory, in every laugh, in every step forward."

Alternative Closing: "Some friendships never end, even in death. Rest well, my dear friend - you will always be with me."

9. A Friend Who Was Like a Sibling

Opening: "Some friendships go beyond companionship - they become family. [Name] was not just my friend, but my sibling in every way that mattered. Today, I honour the life of someone who shaped my world with love, laughter, and unwavering support."

Alternative Opening: "There are friends, and then there are those rare people who become a part of your soul. [Name] was one of those people for me. Though we were not related by blood, our bond was as strong as any family connection."

Middle: "From the first moment we met, I knew [Name] was special. [Share a story of how your friendship began or a defining moment that solidified your bond.]"

"Through every triumph and every hardship, [Name] was by my side. [Describe a time they supported you, a lesson they taught you, or a challenge you faced together.]"

"Their love, their humour, their unwavering presence - these are the things I will cherish forever. [Reflect on what made them unique and irreplaceable.]"

Closing: "Though I grieve today, I take comfort in knowing that true friendships never end. [Name] will always be a part of me, in my heart and in my memories."

Alternative Closing: "This is not a goodbye; this is a promise to carry forward the love, the laughter, and the light [Name] brought into my life."

10. A Lifelong Bond That Time Cannot Break

Opening: "Few people are lucky enough to find a friend who lasts a lifetime. I was blessed to have [Name] - a friend who was with me through every stage of life, who stood beside me in every joy and sorrow."

Alternative Opening: "Life gives us many acquaintances, but very few true friends. [Name] was that true friend - one who never wavered, who always showed up, and who filled my life with love."

Middle: "We had a lifetime of memories together. [Share a story of a moment that captures the depth of your friendship.]"

"No matter the miles between us, no matter how time passed, our bond never changed. [Describe the unbreakable nature of your friendship and the moments that defined it.]"

"[Name] had a way of making life feel lighter, even in its heaviest moments. [Reflect on how they supported you, the joy they brought, and the mark they left on your heart.]"

Closing: "Though I will miss [Name] every single day, I take comfort in knowing that love like this never truly ends. Their presence will remain with me in every memory, every story, and every laugh we once shared."

Alternative Closing: "Friendships like ours don't fade with time or distance. I will hold [Name] in my heart forever, and until we meet again, I will honour them by living as they did - with love, kindness, and joy."

Chapter 13

FOR UNEXPECTED OR TRAGIC DEATHS

1. A Life Taken Too Soon (For Accidents and Sudden Loss)

Opening: "Today, we gather with heavy hearts to remember [Name], whose time with us was far too short. The suddenness of [his/her] passing has left us all in shock, struggling to find meaning in this loss. But even in sorrow, we must also celebrate the incredible life [Name] lived."

Alternative Opening: "There are no words to fully capture the depth of our grief today. [Name] was here one moment and gone the next, and our hearts are aching in ways we never imagined. But as we mourn, we also remember - a life that brought so much joy, so much love, and so many unforgettable moments."

Middle: "[Name] lived with passion, kindness, and a heart full of love. [Share a special memory - whether about their adventurous spirit, generosity, or the way they brightened the lives of others.]"

"Though [his/her] time with us was far too brief, the impact [he/she] made on this world will last forever. [Describe how they influenced friends, family, or their community.]"

"It is hard to accept that [he/she] is no longer with us, but I choose to hold on to the laughter, the love, and the moments we shared. [Reflect on a personal story that brings light in this dark moment.]"

Closing: "Though we were not ready to say goodbye, we must carry [Name]'s love and spirit with us. Let us honour [his/her] memory by living as [he/she] did - with kindness, courage, and joy."

Alternative Closing: "Loss this sudden is unfair and painful, but love does not fade with time. As we say goodbye today, we promise to remember, to honour, and to keep [Name]'s memory alive in our hearts."

2. A Gentle Soul Lost to Mental Health Struggles
(For Suicide and Mental Health Considerations)

Opening: "Today, we gather not just to grieve the loss of [Name], but to remember the light [he/she] brought into our lives. Though we wish we could have eased [his/her] pain, we take comfort in knowing [he/she] is now at peace."

Alternative Opening: "Mental health struggles can feel invisible to the outside world, yet they are so real and heavy to bear. [Name] carried a burden we may never fully understand, but today we do not focus on [his/her] struggles - we focus on the love, the kindness, and the life that deserves to be honoured."

Middle: "[Name] was a person of depth, emotion, and compassion. [Share a story that reflects their kindness, humour, or the way they made others feel seen and valued.]"

"Though [he/she] faced struggles, [he/she] also shared joy. [Reflect on a time when they made someone smile or pursued their passions.]"

"If there is one thing we must remember, it is that [Name] was so much more than [his/her] pain. [Speak about their legacy - the love they gave, the friendships they built, and the lessons they leave behind.]"

Closing: "While we wish for more time, we choose to celebrate the time we were given. [Name]'s story does not end today, because we will carry [his/her] memory forward."

Alternative Closing: "Let us honour [Name] by spreading the love [he/she] so freely gave. Let us be gentle with each other, and let us never forget the beauty [he/she] brought into this world."

3. The Struggles of Addiction Do Not Define a Life *(For Overdose and Addiction-Related Loss)*

Opening: "Addiction is a battle, one that too many face, and one that we wish had not taken [Name] from us. But today, we do not define [him/her] by this struggle - we define [him/her] by the love, the laughter, and the incredible person [he/she] was."

Alternative Opening: "The weight of addiction can feel insurmountable, but it never defined [Name]. [He/She] was a person of love, of resilience, of hope. And that is who we remember today."

Middle: "[Name] had a heart bigger than the world. [Share a memory of their kindness, generosity, or the unique way they touched lives.]"

"Though [his/her] journey was not easy, [he/she] never stopped loving, never stopped trying, and never stopped being someone who mattered. [Reflect on a story that shows their strength and perseverance.]"

"[He/She] may have faced struggles, but [he/she] also brought joy. [Describe a time when they were happiest, and how they made others feel.]"

Closing: "We will not remember [Name] for how [he/she] left us - we will remember [him/her] for how [he/she] lived. That is the story we hold onto today."

Alternative Closing: "Though addiction took [Name] too soon, love is stronger than loss. And so we will carry [his/her] love with us, always."

4. A Light Extinguished Too Soon (For Young Lives Lost Unexpectedly)

Opening: "There are losses that shake us to our core, and today we grieve one of those. [Name] was taken from us far too soon, and while we struggle to understand, we also hold onto the love and joy [he/she] brought into our lives."

Alternative Opening: "No words can ease the pain we feel today. The loss of [Name] is beyond comprehension, and yet, in our grief, we choose to remember the light [he/she] shared with the world."

Middle: "[Name] was full of life, laughter, and kindness. [Share a memory that highlights their spirit, their dreams, or their unique presence.]"

"Though their time was brief, their impact was immeasurable. [Reflect on how they touched lives and made the world a better place.]"

Closing: "Though we may never understand why [Name] was taken so soon, we will forever carry their love and legacy in our hearts."

Alternative Closing: "We honour [Name] not by dwelling on what was lost, but by cherishing what was given - the love, the joy, and the time we were blessed to share."

5. A Love That Transcends Loss *(For Any Unexpected Passing)*

Opening: "Grief is the price we pay for love, and today we feel that deeply. [Name] was taken from us suddenly, but the love [he/she] left behind will never fade."

Alternative Opening: "There are no words to make sense of this loss. But while [Name] may be gone, [his/her] love remains, woven into the lives of all who knew [him/her]."

Middle: "The impact of [Name]'s life was immeasurable. [Share a memory that speaks to their love, their kindness, or the legacy they leave behind.]"

Closing: "Love does not end, and neither does memory. We will hold [Name] close in our hearts, today and always."

FOR DEATH DUE TO ILLNESS

1. A Tribute to Strength and Resilience *(For Someone Who Fought a Long Illness)*

Opening: "Today, we gather to honour the life of [Name], who faced illness with unwavering strength and an unbreakable spirit. [His/Her] journey was not defined by sickness, but by the love, resilience, and courage [he/she] showed every single day."

Alternative Opening: "Even in the midst of illness, [Name] taught us all what it meant to persevere. Though we grieve today, we also celebrate a life lived with extraordinary strength and dignity."

Middle: "Through all the challenges, [Name] remained a beacon of hope. [Share a story of their bravery, their determination, or how they lifted others despite their struggles.]"

"[He/She] never let illness define [him/her], choosing instead to embrace life's joys whenever possible. [Reflect on a moment of laughter, love, or resilience that embodies their spirit.]"

"To know [Name] was to witness true courage. [Speak about the example they set for family, friends, and all who knew them.]"

Closing: "Though illness took [Name] from us, it never took away [his/her] spirit. We will forever hold onto the love, the lessons, and the strength [he/she] gave us."

Alternative Closing: "May we honour [Name] by facing our own challenges with the same grace and resilience [he/she] showed us all."

2. Battling Long-Term Illness with Courage *(For Someone Who Endured Years of Illness)*

Opening: "It is never easy to watch a loved one battle illness, but [Name] faced each day with courage and unwavering faith. Today, we remember [him/her] not for the struggle, but for the life, love, and inspiration [he/she] shared with all of us."

Alternative Opening: "[Name] was a fighter - not just in illness, but in life. No matter how difficult the road, [he/she] never gave up hope, never stopped loving, and never let go of [his/her] joy."

Middle: "Even when times were tough, [Name] found ways to brighten our lives. [Share a memory of their humour, kindness, or determination.]"

"[He/She] taught us the meaning of perseverance. [Describe how they faced their illness and the example they set for others.]"

"Though illness took a toll, it never dimmed [his/her] light. [Reflect on how they continued to inspire and love despite their struggles.]"

Closing: "[Name] may no longer be with us, but the love and lessons [he/she] left behind will never fade. We will carry [his/her] spirit forward in all we do."

Alternative Closing: "As we say goodbye today, let us promise to honour [Name] by embracing life with the same courage [he/she] showed us every day."

3. Acknowledging the Pain and Finding Peace (For Someone Who Fought Bravely But Suffered Deeply)

Opening: "Some battles are longer than we wish, and some burdens are heavier than we can bear. [Name] faced [his/her] illness with more strength than most could ever imagine, and though our hearts are heavy today, we take solace in knowing [he/she] is at peace."

Alternative Opening: "Illness is unfair, but [Name] never let it steal [his/her] kindness, [his/her] laughter, or [his/her] love for the people in [his/her] life. Today, we remember the joy [he/she] shared with us, even in the face of hardship."

Middle: "[Name] endured so much, yet never stopped loving, never stopped hoping, and never stopped fighting. [Share a story about their strength, their determination, or their ability to find light in the darkest times.]"

"While we mourn today, we also find comfort in knowing [his/her] suffering has ended. [Reflect on how they wished for peace, and how they now rest free from pain.]"

"[Name] would not want us to dwell in sorrow but to cherish the good memories, the laughter, and the love [he/she] left behind."

Closing: "Though we grieve, we take comfort in knowing [Name] is finally at peace. May we carry [his/her] love with us always."

Alternative Closing: "[Name]'s battle has ended, but [his/her] impact on our lives will never fade. Let us honour [him/her] by finding light even in the darkest moments."

4. The Grace of Letting Go (For Someone Who Accepted Their Fate with Peace)

Opening: "Some face their final days with fear, but [Name] met them with grace. [He/She] taught us all the meaning of peace and acceptance, reminding us that love is eternal and life is to be cherished."

Alternative Opening: "[Name] knew that life is not measured by years, but by love. Even in the face of illness, [he/she] continued to share warmth, wisdom, and unwavering faith."

Middle: "[Name] spent [his/her] final days reminding us to treasure every moment. [Share a story of their wisdom, their acts of love, or a special goodbye.]"

"[He/She] found peace in knowing that love does not fade, and today we hold on to that truth. [Reflect on their final messages, hopes, or words of comfort.]"

Closing: "Though we say farewell, we know [Name] is free from pain and watching over us."

Alternative Closing: "Let us honour [Name] not by mourning, but by living as [he/she] did - with grace, love, and gratitude."

5. A Warrior's Goodbye (For Someone Who Fought Until the End)

Opening: "[Name] was a warrior in every sense of the word. Through pain, through hardship, through uncertainty, [he/she] fought with every ounce of strength [he/she] had. Today, we honour that courage."

Middle: "[Name] never backed down from a challenge, not even when faced with [his/her] greatest battle. [Share a story that exemplifies their strength and determination.]"

"Though we wish [he/she] had more time, we are grateful for the love and lessons [he/she] gave us."

Closing: "[Name] may be gone, but the fight [he/she] waged, the love [he/she] shared, and the memories we hold will never fade."

6. Finding Light in the Darkness (For Someone Whose Spirit Never Dimmed)

Opening: "Even in suffering, [Name] found reasons to smile, to love, and to believe in tomorrow. Today, we celebrate a life that was full of light, even in the darkest moments."

Middle: "[Name] refused to let illness take away [his/her] joy. [Share a story of their optimism, their kindness, or their ability to inspire.]"

Closing: "Though [he/she] is no longer with us, [his/her] light will never fade. We will carry it with us, always."

FOR THE ELDERLY WHO LIVED A FULL LIFE

1. A Life Well-Lived (For Someone Who Embraced Every Moment)

Opening: "Today, we gather not just to mourn the passing of [Name], but to celebrate a life well-lived. [He/She] lived fully, loved deeply, and left behind a legacy that will endure in all of us."

Alternative Opening: "A long life is not measured by years alone, but by the love shared, the wisdom imparted, and the lives touched. [Name] was a person who filled every moment with purpose."

Middle: "[Name] lived life with passion, embracing every experience with joy and determination. [Share a story about their adventures, passions, or defining moments.]"

"Through challenges and triumphs alike, [he/she] remained steadfast in [his/her] values. [Reflect on a lesson they taught or a belief they held dear.]"

"Family and friends were at the heart of [Name]'s journey, and [his/her] love will live on through each of us. [Describe how they nurtured those around them.]"

Closing: "While we say goodbye today, we do so with gratitude. [Name] lived a full life, and we are blessed to have been part of it."

Alternative Closing: "Though [he/she] is gone, [his/her] spirit lives on in the love and lessons [he/she] shared. May we carry that love forward."

2. A Legacy of Wisdom and Love (For a Grandparent or Elder Who Taught and Inspired)

Opening: "Few people leave behind a legacy as rich as [Name]'s. A source of wisdom, kindness, and unwavering love, [he/she] shaped the lives of so many."

Alternative Opening: "We are here today not just to say goodbye to [Name], but to honour a lifetime of lessons, laughter, and love."

Middle: "[Name] was a storyteller, a teacher, and a guide. [Share a lesson they imparted or a tradition they upheld.]"

"Through every challenge, [he/she] remained a steady presence, always offering love and support. [Describe a time when their wisdom helped others.]"

"[Name]'s impact will be felt for generations, as we carry forward the values and love [he/she] instilled in us."

Closing: "Though [he/she] is no longer with us, [his/her] love remains. We honour [Name] today by living the way [he/she] taught us to."

Alternative Closing: "Let us cherish the memories and lessons of [Name], ensuring [his/her] light never fades."

3. A Peaceful Farewell (For Someone Who Passed Peacefully in Old Age)

Opening: "Today, we say farewell to [Name], who left this world as gently as [he/she] lived in it. A life well-lived, full of love and kindness, deserves to be honoured with joy as much as sorrow."

Alternative Opening: "There is a certain beauty in a life that has run its full course, a life lived with grace and meaning. Today, we remember [Name] and celebrate the peace [he/she] found in [his/her] final days."

Middle: "[Name] embraced life with a quiet strength, always offering wisdom and comfort. [Share a memory of their calm presence, their gentle guidance, or their unwavering love.]"

"[He/She] left behind not just memories but a sense of peace, knowing [he/she] had given all the love [he/she] could. [Reflect on their last days and how they prepared for their passing.]"

Closing: "Though we mourn today, we are grateful that [Name] was able to leave this world surrounded by love, just as [he/she] had always lived."

Alternative Closing: "Let us honour [Name] by finding peace in knowing [he/she] lived fully and left behind a legacy of love."

4. A Devoted Parent and Grandparent (For Someone Who Prioritized Family Above All)

Opening: "Family was at the core of [Name]'s life. Every decision, every effort, every moment was dedicated to the love and well-being of those [he/she] cherished most."

Alternative Opening: "[Name] built a life rooted in love, creating a family that flourished under [his/her] care. Today, we honour a life devoted to the ones [he/she] held dear."

Middle: "[Name] found joy in the simplest of moments - family dinners, laughter-filled holidays, and quiet evenings with loved ones. [Share a special memory of their love for family.]"

"[He/She] made everyone feel important, valued, and deeply loved. [Reflect on their impact on children, grandchildren, and extended family.]"

Closing: "Though [Name] is no longer with us, the love [he/she] poured into this family will live on forever."

Alternative Closing: "Family was [his/her] greatest joy, and through us, [he/she] will always be remembered."

5. A Faithful Servant and Community Leader (For Someone Who Lived with Deep Faith and Service)

Opening: "[Name] lived a life of faith, kindness, and unwavering devotion to both family and community. [His/Her] impact reached far beyond the walls of [his/her] home."

Alternative Opening: "To serve others is to lead a life of purpose, and [Name] embodied this every single day. Today, we honour a person of faith, love, and generosity."

Middle: "Whether through church, charity, or simple daily kindness, [Name] uplifted everyone [he/she] met. [Share a story of their generosity or impact.]"

"Faith was [his/her] foundation, and [he/she] lived by its principles every day. [Reflect on how their beliefs shaped their actions and character.]"

Closing: "[Name]'s life was a testimony of faith and love. We honour [his/her] memory by continuing [his/her] good works."

Alternative Closing: "May we walk in [his/her] footsteps, living with the same faith and kindness [he/she] showed us."

6. A Guiding Light for Family and Friends *(For a Wise and Loving Elder)*

Opening: "There are some people whose presence alone is a comfort, whose wisdom is a gift, and whose love makes life richer. [Name] was one of those people."

Alternative Opening: "Today, we honour not just a life, but a guiding light in our family and community. [Name] led with kindness, taught with patience, and loved with all [his/her] heart."

Middle: "[Name] was someone you could always turn to. [Share a personal story that reflects their wisdom and warmth.]"

"Through every stage of life, [he/she] was a steady presence, offering words of encouragement and endless love. [Reflect on their influence on those around them.]"

Closing: "Though [Name] has left this world, [his/her] wisdom will continue to guide us, and [his/her] love will remain in our hearts forever."

Alternative Closing: "We may have lost [Name] in body, but never in spirit. The lessons [he/she] taught us will live on in all we do."

7. A Life of Love and Generosity (For Someone Who Gave Their Heart to Others)

Opening: "Some people give without expecting anything in return. [Name] was one of those rare souls who made the world better simply by being in it."

Alternative Opening: "A person's true legacy is not in what they owned but in how they made others feel. [Name] left behind a legacy of kindness, generosity, and love."

Middle: "[Name] had a heart that never wavered in its devotion to others. [Share an example of their selflessness and compassion.]"

"No matter how much or how little [he/she] had, [he/she] always found a way to give. [Reflect on their charitable nature and the way they uplifted others.]"

Closing: "Though [he/she] is gone, we carry forward [his/her] example of love and generosity in how we treat others."

Alternative Closing: "Let us honour [Name] by living with the same kindness [he/she] showed the world."

8. A Friend to All (For Someone Who Made Everyone Feel Like Family)

Opening: "Some people walk into a room and make everyone feel like family. [Name] had that rare gift - the ability to bring people together with warmth, laughter, and love."

Alternative Opening: "There are those who leave an unforgettable mark on our hearts, not because of what they did, but because of how they made us feel. [Name] was one of those people."

Middle: "No matter who you were or where you came from, [Name] treated everyone with kindness and respect. [Share a moment where their welcoming nature made a difference.]"

"[He/She] had a way of turning acquaintances into friends, and friends into family. [Reflect on their ability to connect with people.]"

Closing: "Though [he/she] is no longer here, the love and friendships [he/she] built will never fade."

Alternative Closing: "[Name] gave us the gift of belonging, and we honour [his/her] memory by carrying that spirit forward."

9. A Life of Laughter and Joy (For Someone Who Lived with Humour and Light-Heartedness)

Opening: "If there's one thing [Name] taught us, it was to find joy in life. Today, we celebrate a person who brought laughter and happiness wherever [he/she] went."

Alternative Opening: "Not everyone gets to live a life full of laughter, but [Name] made sure to find humour even in the smallest moments. Today, we remember [him/her] with smiles, as [he/she] would have wanted."

Middle: "[Name] had a joke for every situation and a way of making life a little lighter. [Share a story of their humour or playfulness.]"

"Even in tough times, [he/she] reminded us that laughter is a gift, and life is meant to be enjoyed."

Closing: "Though [he/she] is gone, we will always hear [his/her] laughter in our hearts."

Alternative Closing: "Let's honour [Name] the way [he/she] lived - with laughter, love, and joy."

10. A Faithful and Loving Spirit (For Someone Whose Life Was Defined by Faith and Love)

Opening: "Faith and love were the cornerstones of [Name]'s life. Today, we celebrate a person who lived with unwavering belief and endless kindness."

Alternative Opening: "[Name] walked in faith and shared [his/her] love freely. As we say goodbye today, we do so knowing [he/she] is at peace."

Middle: "[He/She] lived a life of service, always putting others before [himself/herself]. [Reflect on their selflessness and devotion to faith.]"

Closing: "Though [Name] is now with the Lord, [his/her] love remains in our hearts forever."

11. A Tribute of Respect and Remembrance (For Delivering a Eulogy Without Knowing the Deceased Well)

Opening: "Today, we gather to pay our respects to [Name], a person whose journey through life has now come to an end. While I did not know [him/her] personally, I know that every life carries significance, and every person leaves behind a story worth telling."

Alternative Opening: "We may not always know each other well in life, but in death, we are called to honour and remember. Though I did not have the privilege of knowing [Name] deeply, I stand here today to recognize and respect a life lived."

Middle: "Each of us carries a story, and while I may not have shared in all of [Name]'s moments, I know that [he/she] was part of a greater journey. [Reflect on the impact the person might have had in their community or profession.]"

"In times like these, we reflect on what it means to be human - to love, to experience joy, to leave behind even the smallest acts of kindness that ripple through time. [Name] was part of that shared experience, and today we acknowledge the mark [he/she] left in this world."

Closing: "Though I may not have known [Name] personally, I know that every life matters, and every story deserves to be told. Let us honour [his/her] memory by carrying forward the kindness, respect, and dignity that every human being deserves."

Alternative Closing: "Let us not measure life by how well we knew someone, but by the impact they left behind. May [Name] rest in peace, remembered with dignity and respect."

12. Honouring a Life with Compassion (For When No Family Is Present to Speak)

Opening: "It is never easy to stand in a room where few may have known the one we are here to remember. But every life deserves to be honoured, every passing deserves a farewell. Today, we remember [Name] with compassion, with respect, and with gratitude."

Alternative Opening: "Some lives are filled with large families and gatherings, while others walk a quieter path. No matter the journey, every life is valuable, and today, we stand together to honour [Name]."

Middle: "[Name] was a person who walked this earth, who had joys, struggles, and moments of connection. Though [he/she] may not have had family to stand here today, [his/her] presence mattered. [Reflect on how every person contributes to the world, even in small ways.]"

"We do not measure the worth of a life by the number of people who stand at a service, but by the moments, kindnesses, and legacy left behind. [Name] lived, and that alone is worth remembering."

Closing: "In honouring [Name] today, we affirm that no life goes unnoticed. We acknowledge [his/her] journey and offer our respect and gratitude for a life lived."

FOR PUBLIC FIGURES AND COMMUNITY LEADERS

1. Honouring a Life of Service (For a Public Servant or Political Leader)

Opening: "Today, we gather to honour [Name], a person whose life was dedicated to the service of others. [He/She] believed in the power of leadership, the responsibility of public service, and the importance of standing up for what is right."

Alternative Opening: "The measure of a leader is not in power held, but in the lives changed. [Name] was a servant of the people, a beacon of integrity, and an example of what true leadership looks like."

Middle: "[Name] devoted [his/her] life to the betterment of others, ensuring that every decision, every effort, and every moment of service contributed to a greater good. [Share an example of their leadership and impact.]"

"Beyond titles and responsibilities, [Name] was a person of vision, someone who saw what was possible and worked tirelessly to make it reality. [Reflect on their commitment to progress, justice, or equality.]"

Closing: "Though [he/she] is no longer with us, [his/her] work lives on in the policies enacted, the people inspired, and the change brought forth. We honour [his/her] legacy by continuing the work [he/she] began."

Alternative Closing: "May we remember [Name] not just for the office [he/she] held, but for the hearts [he/she] touched. The world is better because [he/she] was in it."

2. Remembering a Leader, Teacher, or Mentor (For an Educator, Coach, or Community Leader)

Opening: "Some leaders do not seek recognition but lead through example, guidance, and wisdom. [Name] was one of those people - a mentor, a teacher, a light to those who sought knowledge and guidance."

Alternative Opening: "Education is the foundation of progress, and [Name] was a builder of futures. Through patience, encouragement, and unwavering belief in others, [he/she] shaped lives in ways words cannot fully express."

Middle: "[Name] dedicated [his/her] life to empowering others, seeing potential where others saw obstacles. [Share a story of their mentorship, encouragement, or a lesson they imparted.]"

"For [him/her], leadership was not about authority but about impact. [He/She] believed in lifting others, in sharing wisdom freely, and in leaving no one behind."

Closing: "Though [he/she] is gone, the lessons taught, the lives changed, and the wisdom shared will live on. [Name] may no longer be here, but [his/her] influence will endure for generations."

Alternative Closing: "Today, we do not just mourn a leader - we celebrate a legacy. May we take what [Name] taught us and pass it forward, ensuring that [his/her] mission continues."

3. Acknowledging Contributions to Society (For a Humanitarian, Activist, or Philanthropist)

Opening: "The world is shaped by those who dedicate themselves to the well-being of others. Today, we remember [Name], a person whose heart and hands worked tirelessly to build a better future."

Alternative Opening: "Some people live not for themselves, but for the cause of humanity. [Name] was one of those rare souls, dedicating [his/her] life to justice, compassion, and meaningful change."

Middle: "[Name] understood that change does not come through words alone, but through action. [He/She] gave voice to the voiceless, hope to the weary, and courage to those in need. [Share a specific impact of their humanitarian efforts.]"

"Through every act of kindness, every movement for justice, and every life touched, [Name] left behind a legacy of purpose."

Closing: "Though [he/she] is no longer with us, the ripples of [his/her] work will continue to spread. May we honour [his/her] memory by continuing to stand for what is right."

Alternative Closing: "A life of service is a life well-lived. [Name] may have left this world, but [his/her] impact will be felt for generations to come."

4. Celebrating a Visionary (For an Innovator, Artist, or Thinker Who Changed the World)

Opening: "Some people see the world as it is. Others see it as it could be. [Name] was one of those visionaries, someone who refused to accept limitations and instead chose to create."

Alternative Opening: "Innovation is not just about invention - it is about transformation. [Name] challenged the status quo, reshaped perspectives, and left behind a world changed by [his/her] vision."

Middle: "Through [his/her] work, [Name] inspired others to dream bigger, think deeper, and pursue what once seemed impossible. [Share a breakthrough or artistic achievement that defined them.]"

"More than talent, [he/she] had a gift - a way of seeing possibility where others saw obstacles, of bringing new ideas to life in ways that inspired the world."

Closing: "Though [he/she] is no longer with us, [his/her] influence lives on in every idea, every creation, and every life changed by [his/her] work."

Alternative Closing: "May we carry forward [his/her] vision, embracing innovation and creativity as [he/she] did - with boldness and purpose."

5. A Community Pillar (For a Local Leader Who Strengthened Their Community)

Opening: "Communities are built not just by roads and buildings, but by people. [Name] was a cornerstone of our community, dedicating [his/her] life to making it stronger, kinder, and more united."

Alternative Opening: "A true community leader does not seek recognition but gives of themselves so that others may thrive. [Name] was one such person, shaping lives through service, leadership, and love."

Middle: "[Name] worked tirelessly to ensure that no one was forgotten that every voice was heard, and that our town, our home, was a place of opportunity and support. [Share a specific contribution they made to the community.]"

"[He/She] showed us that leadership is not just about making decisions - it is about making a difference. [Reflect on their role in community programs, civic projects, or charitable work.]"

Closing: "Though [Name] is no longer with us, the foundation [he/she] built will remain strong, carried forward by those inspired by [his/her] work."

Alternative Closing: "A community is only as strong as the people who lead it, and [Name] led with heart. May we honour [his/her] legacy by continuing to build and support one another."

6. A Champion on and Off the Field *(For a Beloved Athlete or Coach)*

Opening: "Today, we celebrate the life of [Name], whose passion for [sport] and dedication to excellence inspired so many. But beyond trophies and records, [he/she] was a mentor, a leader, and a champion of the human spirit."

Alternative Opening: "[Name] played the game with heart, but more importantly, [he/she] lived with integrity. [He/She] taught us that true greatness is not just measured in victories but in the lives we uplift along the way."

Middle: "[Name] inspired others not just through skill, but through perseverance, discipline, and sportsmanship. [Share a memorable story of their career or the way they mentored others.]"

"[He/She] left an undeniable mark on the sport and on the people who had the privilege to know [him/her]. [Reflect on the legacy they leave behind.]"

Closing: "Though [Name] has left the game, [his/her] spirit lives on in every athlete, every fan, and every person inspired to push beyond their limits."

Alternative Closing: "The roar of the crowd may fade, but the impact of a true champion lasts forever. Let us honour [Name] by carrying forward [his/her] passion, determination, and love for the game."

7. A Star That Shined Brightly (For an Actor, Musician, or Entertainer)

Opening: "The stage has gone quiet, but the echoes of [Name]'s artistry will never fade. Today, we remember a performer who touched hearts, brought joy, and made the world a little brighter."

Alternative Opening: "Some souls are born to create, to inspire, and to entertain. [Name] had the rare ability to make us feel, to bring us together through music, film, and art."

Middle: "[Name] had a gift that went beyond talent - it was the ability to move people. [Share a story of their greatest performance or the impact they had on fans.]"

"Though [he/she] stood in the spotlight, [Name] always knew that the greatest reward was the love of those who listened, watched, and believed."

Closing: "Though the curtain has closed, [his/her] legacy will live on in every note, every scene, and every heart touched by [his/her] art."

Alternative Closing: "The applause may have ended, but the music, the laughter, and the memories will never fade. [Name]'s star will shine forever."

Part 4: Christian Faith and Eulogies

Chapter 17

INCORPORATING CHRISTIANITY INTO A EULOGY

Christianity provides comfort, hope, and assurance in times of loss. Incorporating Christian elements into a eulogy offers not only a tribute to the departed but also a message of faith for those who grieve. Whether through scripture, prayer, or Christian funeral traditions, faith-centred eulogies remind us of God's promise of eternal life and the power of His love.

1. Choosing Bible Verses, Prayers, or Blessings

A Christian eulogy often includes Bible verses that offer comfort, hope, and reassurance of eternal life. When selecting scripture, consider passages that reflect the character of the deceased and the message you wish to convey. Different verses can provide different messages, such as strength, encouragement, hope, or the promise of everlasting life.

Bible Verses for Comfort:
- **John 14:1-3** – "Do not let your hearts be troubled. You believe in God; believe also in me. My Father's house has many rooms; if that were not so, would I have told you that I am going there to prepare a place for you? And if I go and

prepare a place for you, I will come back and take you to be with me that you also may be where I am."

- **Psalm 23:4** – "Even though I walk through the darkest valley, I will fear no evil, for you are with me; your rod and your staff, they comfort me."

- **2 Corinthians 1:3-4** – "Praise be to the God and Father of our Lord Jesus Christ, the Father of compassion and the God of all comfort, who comforts us in all our troubles, so that we can comfort those in any trouble with the comfort we ourselves receive from God."

Bible Verses for Hope and Eternal Life:

- **1 Thessalonians 4:14** – "For we believe that Jesus died and rose again, and so we believe that God will bring with Jesus those who have fallen asleep in him."

- **Romans 8:38-39** – "For I am convinced that neither death nor life, neither angels nor demons, neither the present nor the future, nor any powers, neither height nor depth, nor anything else in all creation, will be able to separate us from the love of God that is in Christ Jesus our Lord."

- **Revelation 21:4** – "He will wipe every tear from their eyes. There will be no more death or mourning or crying or pain, for the old order of things has passed away."

Prayers and Blessings to Include: Including a prayer or blessing in a eulogy allows mourners to find comfort in faith. A simple yet powerful prayer can help transition the eulogy to a moment of reflection or peace.

Example Closing Prayer: "Heavenly Father, we give thanks for the life of [Name]. We ask for Your comfort as we grieve, and we trust in Your promise of eternal life. May [his/her] soul find rest in

Your presence, and may we carry forward the love and faith [he/she] shared with us. Amen."

Example Blessing for the Departed: "May the Lord bless you and keep you; may His face shine upon you and be gracious to you; may the Lord turn His face toward you and give you peace." (Numbers 6:24-26)

2. Honouring Christian Funeral Traditions

Christian funerals follow sacred traditions that celebrate the life of the departed while acknowledging the promise of resurrection. When writing a eulogy, consider incorporating elements that align with these customs.

Common Christian Funeral Elements:

- **A Message of Hope:** Christians believe in eternal life through Christ. A eulogy should reflect this assurance with words of faith and trust in God's plan. Example: "Though we grieve today, we do not grieve as those who have no hope, for we believe that [Name] is now with the Lord in eternal peace."

- **References to God's Love:** Speak of God's mercy, grace, and unending love, offering reassurance to those in mourning. Example: "God's love is steadfast and unchanging, and even in our sorrow, He walks with us."

- **Personal Testimony of Faith:** If the deceased was a devoted Christian, share stories of their faith, service, and how they lived according to God's will.

- **Mention of Christian Sacraments:** If applicable, reference their baptism, communion, or active role in the church. Example: "From the moment of [his/her] baptism,

[Name] lived in the grace of God and carried that light throughout life."

3. Personalizing Faith-Based Eulogies

A faith-centred eulogy should feel personal and heartfelt while reflecting Christian values. To tailor the eulogy to the individual, consider:

How did their faith shape their life?

- o Were they a devoted church member, a faithful prayer warrior, or someone who embodied Christ's love in daily actions?

- o Example: "[Name] found peace and purpose in prayer. Every morning, without fail, [he/she] would bow [his/her] head and thank the Lord for another day."

Did they have a favourite Bible verse, hymn, or spiritual saying?

- o Including these elements can make the eulogy deeply personal.

- o Example: "One of [Name]'s favourite hymns was 'Amazing Grace,' and today, as we say goodbye, we hold onto that same grace, knowing we will meet again in God's kingdom."

How did they share their faith with others?

- o Mentioning moments where they encouraged or uplifted others through faith highlights their Christian legacy.

- Example: "[Name] never missed an opportunity to encourage those around [him/her] with words of faith. Whether it was a kind note, a prayer, or simply a warm embrace, [he/she] lived as a testament to God's love."

Did they find comfort in a particular Christian teaching?

- If so, reflecting on this can offer peace and hope to mourners.

- Example: "[Name] always spoke of the power of faith in difficult times, often saying, 'Trust in the Lord with all your heart and lean not on your own understanding' (Proverbs 3:5)."

Example Personal Reflection: "[Name] lived each day with unwavering faith, always turning to God in times of joy and trial. [He/She] often shared [his/her] favourite verse, '[Insert Bible Verse],' reminding us that God's love never fails. We find comfort today knowing that [Name] has been welcomed into the arms of our Savior."

> Incorporating Christianity into a eulogy ensures that the words spoken honour both the life of the departed and the eternal hope found in Christ. A Christian eulogy is a way to celebrate not only the memories left behind but also the promise of a heavenly reunion. It allows us to grieve with hope, knowing that through Christ, death is not the end but the beginning of eternal life. May every word spoken be filled with love, faith, and the assurance that we will one day meet again in His presence.

Chapter 18

BIBLE VERSES FOR WRITING YOUR EULOGY

The Bible offers words of comfort, hope, and encouragement in times of grief. Scripture reassures us of God's love, the promise of eternal life, and the peace that surpasses all understanding. Whether used to open, close, or provide reflection within a eulogy, Bible verses serve as a powerful reminder of faith and the journey beyond this life. Below is a selection of scriptures that can bring solace to mourners and honour the departed.

1. Scriptures of Comfort and Hope

When we experience loss, we often seek comfort in God's Word. These passages remind us of His unfailing presence and love during our moments of sorrow.

Psalm 34:18 – "The Lord is close to the broken-hearted and saves those who are crushed in spirit."

Matthew 5:4 – "Blessed are those who mourn, for they will be comforted."

Isaiah 41:10 – "So do not fear, for I am with you; do not be dismayed, for I am your God. I will strengthen you and help you; I will uphold you with my righteous right hand."

2 Corinthians 1:3-4 – "Praise be to the God and Father of our Lord Jesus Christ, the Father of compassion and the God of all comfort, who comforts us in all our troubles, so that we can comfort those in any trouble with the comfort we ourselves receive from God."

John 16:22 – "So with you: Now is your time of grief, but I will see you again and you will rejoice, and no one will take away your joy."

Lamentations 3:31-32 – "For no one is cast off by the Lord forever. Though he brings grief, he will show compassion, so great is his unfailing love."

2. Verses on Eternal Life and Peace

Christians believe that death is not the end but the beginning of eternal life with God. These scriptures affirm the hope of resurrection, and the peace found in God's promise of salvation.

John 11:25-26 – "Jesus said to her, 'I am the resurrection and the life. The one who believes in me will live, even though they die; and whoever lives by believing in me will never die.'"

Romans 6:5 – "For if we have been united with him in a death like his, we will certainly also be united with him in a resurrection like his."

Philippians 3:20-21 – "But our citizenship is in heaven. And we eagerly await a Savior from there, the Lord Jesus Christ, who, by the power that enables him to bring everything under his control, will transform our lowly bodies so that they will be like his glorious body."

Revelation 21:4 – "He will wipe every tear from their eyes. There will be no more death or mourning or crying or pain, for the old order of things has passed away."

1 Corinthians 15:54-55 – "When the perishable has been clothed with the imperishable, and the mortal with immortality, then the saying that is written will come true: 'Death has been swallowed up in victory.' Where, O death, is your victory? Where, O death, is your sting?"

2 Timothy 4:7-8 – "I have fought the good fight, I have finished the race, I have kept the faith. Now there is in store for me the crown of righteousness, which the Lord, the righteous Judge, will award to me on that day - and not only to me, but also to all who have longed for his appearing."

3. Encouraging Words for Those in Mourning

For those left behind, grief can feel overwhelming. These Bible verses offer encouragement and remind us that God is our refuge and strength in difficult times.

Psalm 46:1-2 – "God is our refuge and strength, an ever-present help in trouble. Therefore, we will not fear, though the earth give way and the mountains fall into the heart of the sea."

Isaiah 25:8 – "He will swallow up death forever. The Sovereign Lord will wipe away the tears from all faces; he will remove his people's disgrace from all the earth. The Lord has spoken."

Deuteronomy 31:8 – "The Lord himself goes before you and will be with you; he will never leave you nor forsake you. Do not be afraid; do not be discouraged."

Psalm 73:26 – "My flesh and my heart may fail, but God is the strength of my heart and my portion forever."

2 Thessalonians 2:16-17 – "May our Lord Jesus Christ himself and God our Father, who loved us and by his grace gave us eternal encouragement and good hope, encourage your hearts and strengthen you in every good deed and word."

Hebrews 6:19 – "We have this hope as an anchor for the soul, firm and secure."

4. Bible Verses for Specific Eulogy Themes

Sometimes, a eulogy may have a specific theme depending on the life of the departed. These verses can be used to reflect their character and legacy.

For a Faithful Servant of God:

Matthew 25:23 – "His master replied, 'Well done, good and faithful servant! You have been faithful with a few things; I will put you in charge of many things. Come and share your master's happiness!'"

Psalm 116:15 – "Precious in the sight of the Lord is the death of his faithful servants."

For a Loving Parent or Grandparent:

Proverbs 22:6 – "Start children off on the way they should go, and even when they are old they will not turn from it."

Exodus 20:12 – "Honour your father and your mother, so that you may live long in the land the Lord your God is giving you."

For a Person of Strength and Character:

Joshua 1:9 – "Have I not commanded you? Be strong and courageous. Do not be afraid; do not be discouraged, for the Lord your God will be with you wherever you go."

Proverbs 31:25 – "She is clothed with strength and dignity; she can laugh at the days to come."

For Someone Who Inspired Others:

Hebrews 13:7 – "Remember your leaders, who spoke the word of God to you. Consider the outcome of their way of life and imitate their faith."

Daniel 12:3 – "Those who are wise will shine like the brightness of the heavens, and those who lead many to righteousness, like the stars for ever and ever."

The Bible offers profound words of encouragement, faith, and hope for those who grieve. Whether used as the foundation of a eulogy or simply as a moment of reflection, these scriptures remind us that death is not the end but a transition into God's eternal kingdom. As we honour our loved ones, let us cling to the promises found in His Word, drawing strength from His love and the knowledge that we will be reunited one day in His glory.

Part 5: Additional Guidance & Resources

Chapter 19

HANDLING GRIEF AND LOSS

Grief is a deeply personal experience that affects each person differently. Losing a loved one brings emotional, spiritual, and even physical challenges that require time and support to process. Understanding the grieving process and finding effective coping strategies can help individuals navigate their loss while honouring the memory of the departed.

1. Understanding the Grieving Process

Grief is not a linear process, and there is no right or wrong way to experience it. However, many people find that their grief follows a pattern of emotions and responses. The well-known Kübler-Ross model outlines **five stages of grief**:

- **Denial:** A state of shock or disbelief that the loss has occurred. It may feel surreal or impossible to accept.
- **Anger:** Feelings of frustration, injustice, or resentment toward the situation, others, or even God.
- **Bargaining:** An attempt to regain control by making promises or wishing for things to be different.
- **Depression:** A deep sadness that sets in when the reality of the loss becomes fully acknowledged.
- **Acceptance:** Coming to terms with the loss, allowing healing to begin.

While these stages provide a framework, not everyone will experience them in order or in the same way. Some may cycle through stages multiple times, while others may not experience certain stages at all. Grief is unique to each individual and should be met with compassion and patience.

According to the University of Utah Health, acknowledging and embracing emotions is essential. Suppressing feelings can hinder the healing process. They emphasize the importance of allowing oneself to feel the complex emotions that accompany loss *(https://accelerate.uofuhealth.utah.edu/resilience/grief-in-healthcare-understanding-and-coping)*.

Common Emotional and Physical Responses to Grief:

- o Feeling overwhelmed or numb
- o Experiencing mood swings or emotional outbursts
- o Physical exhaustion or trouble sleeping
- o Changes in appetite
- o Feelings of loneliness or isolation
- o Deep reflection on the past and shared memories

Understanding that grief is a process, not a destination, can help individuals navigate their loss without feeling pressured to "move on" too quickly.

2. Coping Strategies for the Bereaved

Coping with grief is a personal journey, but there are several strategies that can help ease the burden and provide comfort during this difficult time.

A. Lean on Faith and Prayer

For those who find solace in faith, turning to prayer, scripture, and church communities can be a powerful way to process grief. Reading passages that reinforce God's love and the promise of eternal life can bring peace.

Suggested Bible Verses for Comfort:

- **Psalm 147:3** – "He heals the broken-hearted and binds up their wounds."
- **Matthew 11:28** – "Come to me, all who labor and are heavy laden, and I will give you rest."
- **Romans 15:13** – "May the God of hope fill you with all joy and peace in believing, so that by the power of the Holy Spirit you may abound in hope."

Prayer can also serve as a means of expressing grief, asking for strength, and feeling God's presence in times of sorrow.

Example Prayer for Healing: "Lord, in my sorrow, I seek Your comfort. Be my refuge, my strength, and my peace. Help me to trust in Your plan, knowing that my loved one is safe in Your eternal embrace. Amen."

B. Seek Support from Loved Ones and Community

Grief can be an isolating experience, but no one should have to endure it alone. Connecting with family, friends, and support groups can provide much-needed encouragement and companionship.

The National Institutes of Health (NIH) advises talking with caring friends and letting others know when support is needed. Their research highlights that sharing feelings with trusted individuals can provide comfort and aid in processing grief *(https://newsinhealth.nih.gov/2017/10/coping-grief)*.

Ways to seek support:

- Talk to a trusted friend or family member about your emotions.
- Join a grief support group through a church or community centre.
- Consider speaking with a counsellor or pastor who can offer guidance and biblical encouragement.

Being around people who understand the weight of loss can make a significant difference in the healing process.

C. Express Grief Through Journaling and Reflection

Writing about emotions, memories, and prayers can be a helpful way to process grief. A journal provides a safe space to explore feelings, document thoughts, and reflect on cherished moments with the deceased.

Journaling Prompts for Healing:

- What is a favourite memory I have of my loved one?
- How did my loved one impact my faith or perspective on life?
- What are three things I am grateful for today, despite my sorrow?

Journaling can be a therapeutic practice that helps the bereaved process emotions in a personal and meaningful way.

D. Engage in Meaningful Rituals to Honour the Departed

Many find comfort in engaging in small, meaningful rituals that celebrate the life of their loved one. Some ideas include:

- Lighting a candle in remembrance.
- Creating a scrapbook of cherished moments and photos.
- Volunteering or donating to a cause important to the deceased.
- Planting a tree or flower in their memory.

These actions serve as gentle reminders that love transcends loss and that the memory of the departed continues to live on.

E. Allow Yourself Time and Grace to Heal

Grief does not have a set timeline. Healing happens at its own pace, and it is important to allow oneself to experience all emotions without judgment or pressure.

The National Center for Biotechnology Information (NCBI) recommends activities such as prayer, meditation, exercise, art, and music to help individuals progress through their grief journey *(https://www.ncbi.nlm.nih.gov/books/NBK591827/)*.

- Do not rush the process - grief takes time.
- Be patient and kind to yourself.

- o Seek moments of peace through nature, music, or quiet prayer.
- o Remember that healing does not mean forgetting but learning to carry the love forward.

The NIH also emphasizes the importance of regular exercise, a balanced diet, and adequate sleep. They caution against habits that may jeopardize health, such as excessive alcohol consumption or smoking, which can sometimes become coping mechanisms *(https://newsinhealth.nih.gov/2017/10/coping-grief)*.

For those struggling to cope, seeking professional assistance can be beneficial. The Substance Abuse and Mental Health Services Administration (SAMHSA) provides resources for healthcare practitioners to help individuals manage grief after traumatic events (https://library.samhsa.gov/sites/default/files/sma17-5036.pdf).

Grief is one of life's greatest challenges, but through faith, support, and intentional coping strategies, healing is possible. God walks alongside us in our pain, offering comfort and hope through His Word and His presence. As we navigate loss, let us hold onto His promises and cherish the memories that keep our loved ones close in spirit.

"For I consider that the sufferings of this present time are not worth comparing with the glory that is to be revealed to us." – Romans 8:18

FUNERAL ETIQUETTE AND TYPICAL TRADITIONS

Funerals serve as a time for remembrance, mourning, and honouring the life of a loved one. They are sacred events filled with emotion, ritual, and tradition. Understanding funeral etiquette ensures that attendees show respect for the deceased, their family, and the customs of the service. This chapter explores what to expect at a funeral and how to offer condolences in a meaningful and respectful manner.

1. What to Expect at a Funeral

Every funeral is unique, shaped by the traditions, culture, and religious beliefs of the family. However, there are common elements in most services that attendees can expect.

A. The Structure of a Funeral Service

Funerals may vary, but they typically follow a structured format, including:

- **A Gathering and Welcome:** Family and friends arrive, offering quiet support and comforting one another.

- **Opening Words or Prayers:** Often led by a religious leader, minister, or celebrant, the service begins with a message of remembrance and comfort.

- **Eulogies and Tributes:** Loved ones may speak about the deceased, sharing memories, stories, and reflections on their life.

- **Readings and Hymns:** Bible verses, prayers, poetry, or hymns may be included as a way to honour the deceased's faith and beliefs.

- **The Closing and Farewell:** The service may conclude with final words of blessing, a prayer, or a symbolic ritual such as releasing doves, lighting candles, or placing flowers.

- **The Procession and Burial (If Applicable):** In traditional services, the casket may be transported to a burial site or a final resting place, where another short ceremony may take place.

B. Religious and Cultural Variations

Different faiths and cultures have distinct funeral customs. Understanding these differences is essential for showing respect.

- **Christian Funerals:** Often include scripture readings, hymns, and a message of resurrection and eternal life. A priest or minister typically leads the service.

- **Catholic Funerals:** May involve a full Mass, prayers for the deceased's soul, and rites such as the sprinkling of holy water.

- **Jewish Funerals:** Typically held shortly after death, with readings from the Hebrew Scriptures and a graveside service. Shiva, a mourning period, follows the burial.

- **Muslim Funerals:** Include washing of the body, prayers at the mosque, and burial facing Mecca. Cremation is prohibited.

- **Secular or Non-Religious Funerals:** May be led by a celebrant and focus on honouring the deceased's life through personal stories and readings rather than religious elements.

Understanding and respecting these customs ensures that you approach the funeral with the right level of decorum and sensitivity.

2. How to Offer Condolences Respectfully

Offering condolences is an important part of showing support to the grieving family. However, it is important to do so in a way that is appropriate and considerate.

A. Expressing Sympathy in Person

When attending a funeral or wake, keep your words brief but heartfelt. Some comforting phrases include:

- "I'm so sorry for your loss. [Name] was a wonderful person."
- "My heart goes out to you during this difficult time."
- "If there's anything I can do, please don't hesitate to ask."

A gentle handshake, a hug (if appropriate), or a quiet nod can also convey support when words feel inadequate.

B. Writing a Sympathy Card or Letter

A written message allows you to offer condolences in a more personal and lasting way. When writing a sympathy card:

- Express your sorrow for the loss.

- Share a fond memory or reflection about the deceased.
- Offer comfort and let them know they are in your prayers.
- Keep it simple and sincere.

Example: "Dear [Name], I was heartbroken to hear about the passing of [Deceased's Name]. I will always remember [his/her] kindness and the way [he/she] made everyone feel welcome. Please know that I am keeping you and your family in my prayers. May God bring you comfort and peace during this difficult time."

C. Offering Help and Support

Grieving families often struggle with daily tasks while mourning. Offering specific help can be more meaningful than a general statement.

Instead of saying, "Let me know if you need anything," consider saying:

- "I would love to drop off a meal for your family this week. Would Wednesday be okay?"
- "I'm happy to help with errands or childcare if you need it."
- "I can pick up groceries or take care of some household chores if that would be helpful."

Being proactive in offering assistance can lighten the burden for those in mourning.

D. What Not to Say

Even with the best intentions, some phrases may be hurtful or dismissive to those grieving. Avoid saying:

- "They are in a better place."
- "At least they lived a long life."
- "Everything happens for a reason."
- "I know exactly how you feel."
- "You should be strong for your family."

Grief is personal, and there is no right way to process it. Simply being present and offering compassionate support is more valuable than trying to offer explanations.

> Understanding funeral etiquette and offering condolences with grace and sincerity can provide comfort to those grieving. Funerals are sacred spaces where emotions run deep, and demonstrating respect through thoughtful words and actions can help support those who are mourning. Whether attending a service, writing a sympathy message, or offering assistance, the most important thing is to be present, compassionate, and respectful.

Part 5: Additional Guidance & Resources

Chapter 21

WRITING A PERSONALIZED EULOGY FROM SCRATCH

Writing a eulogy is a deeply personal and emotional task, but it is also a profound way to honour and celebrate the life of a loved one. A well-crafted eulogy provides comfort to those mourning, reflects on the unique personality of the deceased, and ensures that their legacy is remembered with love and respect. This chapter will guide you through the process of crafting a heartfelt and meaningful eulogy, using the Eulogy of Hank as an example of how personal stories and structure can come together.

1. Step-by-Step Guide to Crafting a Unique Eulogy

Writing a eulogy requires thoughtfulness, structure, and sincerity. Below is a step-by-step approach to crafting a compelling and meaningful eulogy.

Step 1: Gather Your Thoughts and Memories

Before you begin writing, take time to reflect on the life of the person you are honouring. Consider the following:

- What were their defining qualities and personality traits?
- What are some memorable stories that highlight who they were?

- How did they impact the lives of those around them?
- Were there any sayings, phrases, or habits that made them unique?
- How would they want to be remembered?

Example: In the case of Hank, he was known for his infectious laughter, love for storytelling, and unwavering kindness. He spent his days teaching and working the farm, caring for his family, and sharing wisdom through small but meaningful gestures.

Step 2: Outline the Structure

A well-organized eulogy follows a clear structure, making it easy for the audience to follow and emotionally connect. A standard eulogy consists of three parts:

- **Introduction:** Welcoming those in attendance, expressing gratitude, and setting the tone.
- **Middle (Body):** Sharing personal stories, memories, and reflections that highlight the deceased's life and values.
- **Conclusion:** Offering words of comfort, summarizing their legacy, and ending on a hopeful or uplifting note.

Step 3: Start with a Warm and Engaging Introduction

Begin the eulogy by introducing yourself and your relationship with the deceased. Express gratitude to those who have gathered to pay their respects.

Example Introduction (Based on Hank's Eulogy): "Good morning, everyone. My name is [Your Name], and it is both an honour and a privilege to stand before you today to celebrate the life of Hank. When I think of Hank, I think of his hearty laugh, the way he always had a story to tell, and how his presence could bring warmth to any room. Today, we gather not only to mourn his passing but to reflect on the incredible life he led and the countless ways he touched our hearts."

Step 4: Share Personal Stories and Memories

The body of the eulogy is where you truly bring the person to life. Use specific anecdotes that highlight their character, humour, generosity, and values.

Example Stories (Expanded from Hank's Eulogy): "Hank was never one to shy away from hard work. He spent his days tending to the farm, ensuring that every acre of land was nurtured with care. But more than his dedication to the land, Hank was dedicated to his family. I remember one summer, the drought had taken its toll, and things were tough. Yet, despite his own worries, Hank insisted on helping his neighbours, sharing what little he had without hesitation."

"One of my favourite memories of Hank was his storytelling. If you ever had the pleasure of sitting with him on the porch at sunset, you'd know that he had a story for every occasion. Whether it was about his childhood adventures, the time he 'accidentally' adopted a stray dog, or the countless pranks he pulled on his brothers, Hank had a way of making the ordinary seem extraordinary."

Adding Humour and Warmth: "Of course, we can't talk about Hank without mentioning his infamous love for milk. If there was ever a man who could drink an entire bottle before sunrise, it was him. And woe to the person who tried to interrupt his morning ritual! But in all seriousness, his love for the simple things in life -

his morning escapade, a good joke, and a well-worn rocking chair - reminded us all to slow down and appreciate the little moments."

Step 5: Conclude with a Meaningful and Hopeful Ending

End the eulogy by summarizing what made the person special, offering a final farewell, and leaving the audience with a message of hope.

Example Conclusion: "Hank lived a life that mattered. Not because of grand achievements or worldly recognition, but because of the love he shared, the lessons he taught, and the laughter he left behind. As we say goodbye today, let us not dwell in sorrow but instead carry forward the light he brought into our lives. May we honour Hank's memory by living as he did - with kindness, laughter, and an open heart."

2. Adding Personal Stories and Memories

A truly impactful eulogy is one that is personal and genuine. To make your eulogy more engaging, consider these techniques:

- **Use vivid details:** Rather than simply saying, "Hank was kind," illustrate his kindness through a story.
- **Incorporate humour where appropriate:** Light-hearted moments can bring warmth and celebration to the eulogy.
- **Speak from the heart:** Authenticity is more powerful than perfection. Don't worry about making it sound formal - make it real.

If you find yourself struggling to find the right words, consider these prompts:

- o What was the funniest thing they ever did?
- o What was the best piece of advice they ever gave you?
- o What small habits or quirks made them uniquely them?
- o How did they handle challenges or hardships?

Writing a eulogy is a profound responsibility, but it is also a gift - a chance to honour a loved one and share their impact with others. By following this guide, structuring your thoughts, and incorporating heartfelt stories, you can craft a eulogy that not only pays tribute to the person's life but also offers comfort and inspiration to those who hear it.

> As we reflect on my eulogy for Hank, let us remember that a life well-lived is not measured in accolades, but in the love shared, the stories told, and the hearts touched. If you find yourself in the position of writing a eulogy, take a deep breath, speak from the heart, and trust that your words will honour the legacy of the one you cherish.

Chapter 22

FINAL THOUGHTS: THE POWER OF WORDS IN REMEMBRANCE

Words hold immense power, especially when spoken in remembrance of a loved one. A thoughtful eulogy is more than a speech - it is a tribute, a reflection, and a way to keep the spirit of the departed alive in the hearts of those who loved them. As we conclude this book, it is important to reflect on why a well-crafted eulogy matters and how storytelling ensures that the memories of our loved ones never fade.

1. Why a Thoughtful Eulogy Matters

A eulogy is one of the most meaningful ways to honour someone's life. It allows those gathered to remember, reflect, and find comfort in shared memories. A well-prepared eulogy accomplishes several key purposes:

- **Honouring the Deceased:** A eulogy provides an opportunity to highlight the unique qualities, values, and impact of the departed. Whether they were a loving parent, a devoted friend, or an inspiring mentor, their story deserves to be told.
- **Providing Comfort to Mourners:** In times of grief, words can offer solace. A thoughtful eulogy acknowledges the

sorrow of loss while also celebrating the beauty of the life that was lived. By weaving in heartfelt moments and cherished memories, a eulogy reassures mourners that their loved one's presence will endure in spirit.

- o **Creating a Lasting Legacy:** A eulogy is not just about saying goodbye - it is about ensuring that the person's story continues. It becomes a record of their life and values, something that family and friends can look back on as a source of inspiration and connection.

- o **Strengthening the Bonds of Community:** Funerals bring people together, and a well-delivered eulogy can serve as a unifying force. When people hear stories that resonate with their own experiences, it fosters a sense of togetherness and shared remembrance.

Throughout this book, we have explored many ways to structure, personalize, and deliver a eulogy. The examples from Hank's eulogy demonstrated how humour, sincerity, and vivid storytelling can make a eulogy more impactful. The guidance on Christian faith-based eulogies reminded us that for many, faith provides a comforting framework for processing grief. The inclusion of Bible verses and prayers showcased the power of scripture in bringing hope and reassurance.

2. Keeping Memories Alive Through Storytelling

Memories are the threads that connect the past with the present. A well-told story can bring a person's essence back to life, allowing those who hear it to feel their presence once more.

A. The Art of Storytelling in a Eulogy

Storytelling is the heart of a great eulogy. It transforms general reflections into something tangible and personal. When crafting a eulogy, consider these storytelling techniques:

- **Use Specific Details:** Instead of saying, "She was kind," share a moment that illustrates her kindness. Example: "Every winter, she would knit scarves for the neighbourhood children and hand them out just before the first snowfall."

- **Incorporate Humour When Appropriate:** Light-hearted moments provide relief and remind mourners of the joy their loved one brought. Example from Hank's eulogy: His legendary love for milk and the way he could drink an entire bottle before sunrise - small details like these make a eulogy feel alive.

- **Include Personal Anecdotes:** Short, personal stories make a eulogy deeply meaningful. Example: "I remember the time my father spent an entire afternoon teaching me how to ride a bike, running alongside me until he was out of breath. He never gave up on me, and that day taught me more about perseverance than any lecture ever could."

- **Engage the Senses:** Describe scenes vividly to draw the audience in. Example: "The smell of Grandma's freshly baked apple pie would fill the house every Sunday afternoon, a tradition that made us all feel at home."

B. Encouraging Others to Share and Preserve Stories

A eulogy is only the beginning of remembrance. Keeping the memory of a loved one alive requires ongoing storytelling. Here are ways to continue sharing their story:

- **Write Down Memories:** Encourage family members to record their favourite moments in a memory book.

- **Share Stories at Family Gatherings:** Keep the tradition of storytelling alive by retelling favourite anecdotes during holidays or special occasions.

- **Create a Digital Tribute:** Many families find comfort in creating online memorials where loved ones can share photos, messages, and stories.

- **Pass Down Lessons and Traditions:** Honour the legacy of the deceased by continuing the traditions they valued.

As we close this book, let us remember that the words we speak in remembrance hold power. They bring healing, they honour the past, and they offer comfort to the living. Whether you are delivering a eulogy, sharing a memory, or simply reflecting on the life of a loved one, your words keep their spirit alive.

> The process of writing a eulogy is a sacred responsibility - one that requires thoughtfulness, care, and love. But it is also a privilege. It is an opportunity to give voice to a life well lived and to remind those who grieve that love never truly fades.

May we all find the strength to share stories, celebrate memories, and honour the lives of those we hold dear. For in remembrance, they live on.

APPENDIX: BONUS MATERIAL

This appendix includes additional resources to help with the preparation and delivery of a eulogy. Whether you are planning a funeral service, giving a eulogy for the first time, or seeking further reading on grief and healing, this section offers practical tools and guidance.

My Eulogy for Verdon Johns

Read by Jason A. Solomon (author) – Original format 2022

This Eulogy for Verdon was penned by Nerida and Amanda with contributions from many others. Hahahah.

Hopefully, you will be happy to hear I have since edited and refined this essay, for your listening pleasure.

Today, I am humbled by this man. I am honoured to stand here an deliver this Eulogy, this testament to his life, and I will always hold dear to my heart the passion that Verdon had for teaching, and for the quality of life itself. He was, and will remain, the biggest influence in my choosing teaching as my profession. And for this, Uncle Verdon, I thank you.

Verdon David Johns, otherwise known as Verdon, Pop, Mr Johns, Sir, Uncle Verdon, then there's the one his mother gave him----- Verdie and obviously……. Darl.

Reading Verdon's eulogy today, is bittersweet. He was always the person who would write a Eulogy for others and also prepare the order of service.

So Verdon, I know you are listening, hope today is up to your standard mate. And yes it's long…. Hahahah but that's what he would want.

Born at Prince of Wales Hospital in Randwick on the 31st August 1945. The 2nd child of June & Doug, he lived his early years in Randwick and then they moved to Panania (Not Nania with the Lion the Witch and the Wardrobe)

(I actually had to google map that last night. It's some little place buried deep in the west of Sydney between Revesby and Easthills) and this is where he spent his formative childhood and adolescent years.

Family has always been the centre of Verdon's existence. He'd spend the school holidays travelling to Ellalong in the Hunter Valley to spend time with his Grandparents. The family were close to Uncle Eric and Auntie Glady, who were considered his mother's grandparents, as she was taken under their wing because Gran's father died at war.

He attended 2 high schools - finishing year 12 at both Trinity Grammar and East Hills Boys. Apparently his school talents included, but not limited to; and the Jury is still out on this one ……. sprinting, but definitely debating and theatre, cadets, and he was also a surf lifesaver.

Verdon commenced a Law Degree at Sydney Uni, however, pursued his own career pathway, leaving law, and finding himself in teachers college in Wagga 12 months later. Quite possibly this was an unexpected change, for June and Doug!

His teaching career began in good 'Ol ... Gularbambone when he was 23, but as fate would have it, this is when Shirley also came into view. Little did Verdie know, that not only would he fall in love with a local, he would spend the majority of his life .... right there.

Based on quality intel.... Shirley and Verdon's first date, and basically most of the other ones, involved walking to the bowling club, ... in Gulargambone. Being quite the romantic, Verdon took Shirley to a B and S ball at Cobar..... and..... proposed. Upon returning from the B and S ball, Verdon knew he had to ask for permission to marry.

Apparently shirley's sister Norelle knew exactly why Verdon was in the loungeroom, sweating, looking nervous, trying to man up to Mr Hazlett.

Norelle, in what is considered true to her form, refused to leave the loungeroom, just keen to be where the action was! Verdon and Shirley have embraced, enjoyed and treasured a marriage that lasted one lifetime. Their achievements together have seen them buying and building houses, purchasing random blocks of land with friends, studying, completing degrees together and working side by side with their educational tutoring and diverse farming enterprises.

As we all know, Verdon's teaching career started after graduating from Wagga teacher's college back in 1967. Mr Johns .... Or Sir as I called him ...... taught English and History to many willing, hahahah, and not so willing teenagers, spanning more than 40 years.

Verdon also worked at Wyong High School following Gulargambone, where he met some life long friends from the Central Coast, Pam and Geoff, Ian and Sue, and Cecile and Bruce. He later transferred to Dubbo South, then Coonamble and his last official Departmental appointment being at Gilgandra High School.

According to someone, …….. one particular highlight must have been when he was taking the English lesson for Nerida, who was in year 7. Completing a "getting to know you page" plus a spelling assessment……. Verdon was most surprised as he read the first page from the pile ……. Nerida answered the question "What annoys you most?" her written reply "when dad leaves his dirty pyjamas on the kitchen table".

In faith…… he was a titan. Tony Adams described Verdon as a person who "stood with the Lord". Verdon always had a strong Christian faith. He grew up in the Holy Trinity Anglican Church in Panania. Was an active member of the fellowship youth group during this time, and this formed a large part of his social and spiritual endeavours as a young boy growing up. Mick Page, Bob Pithers, Lindon, Russell, Ross, Kay, Sue and Chris were all friends and part of the group. And I'm confident many a funny story from these days can be told.

Verdon re-affirmed his faith as an adult when attending a "Billy Graham ….. Christian rally", which ultimately stoked the fire of his beliefs. His belief in the Lord in his later years was through the unity of christ. To further expand his understanding of the "unity of Christ, he would have regular discussions with Father Martin and he Embraced the ideas of what David, Vivian and Trevor Bell had to offer through their Jehovah Witness teachings. Further, attended the Assemblies of God, Uniting Church and the Aboriginal Inland Mission Church…. and was an active member of the Castlereagh Christian Education Association. In the final weeks or probably months of his life, ….. his life-long spiritual journey and his faith guided and gave him strength to endure the most challenging of struggles. Faithful unto death, ……. Verdon is sure to receive the crown of life.

Here in this Presbyterian Church, many memories have been created. As a Lay Preacher, he delivered sermons and bible readings in this very building, and also in Toorawenah and Gulargambone. Many of us here today were witness to his marriage to Shirley in 1970 on that hot January day. Then the baptism of both Nerida in 1979 and Amanda in 1980, and now …… today ……… …as we remember the life of this spiritual man.

Verdon was a feminist ahead of his time. He was the only male teacher, to take paternity leave, at a time when men were granted 1 week leave after the birth of a baby. Verdon took an additional 3 months off calling it "study leave".

Over the years Verdon has always promoted and supported the careers of his daughters and has been immensely proud of their work in Health. Verdon would even turn up to their work sometimes just to see what they did. One fine day Shirley and Verdon turned up at Dubbo Base Hospital when Amanda was a Locumb. Another time Verdon spent his free day in London tracking down Nerida at her place of employment…. the "Wheelchair Service" in London. This particular effort was rather herculean, as Verdon had absolutely no idea where Nerida worked, but somehow managed to fine her old boss at a different, ……. Much Larger London Hospital, who then sent him in a black taxi to the correct location.

Throughout his life, Verdon was a man who would get involved with many programs – some of them serious, and some of them more light-hearted.

Here's just a sample

- o Involved in fundraising for the Pygmy's in the Congo in early 2000

- o For a few intense months, was convinced he had cracked the code for roulette. Being not much of a gambler, he played on a home roulette wheel. When he finally got to a casino, played a few rounds, won a couple of hundred dollars, and then had to leave. He was so thrilled and excited but worried he was going to get kicked out for cracking the code. Not the Case

- o In retirement from teaching, managed a few projects and called many schools. ie, Verdon and Shirley promoted rural health careers, and preparing for the HSC, they delivered a talk to many country high schools, travelling from town to town as volunteer speakers.

- o He was the master of moving house as Nerida and Amanda have moved houses inumerous times ….. spanning multiple states of Australia.

Public speaking:

We remember growing up that it was always a fight between Pop, Gran and Verdon who would get the microphone or say grace before dinner …. A Party …… funeral …… event or any other large gathering. Verdon was asked to speak at most events … and he took the job seriously. Various singing highlights over the years have included, Roy Orbison at a family holiday and Elvis at Scott's Wedding till the wee hours of the morning.

Verdon's farming career spanned from 1982 until his final weeks… when he still had a plan for the front paddock. Yet if anyone asked him his career….. he was known more as a teacher. Many a family and friend, ……. and it's likely you are in the room right now,……. can remember being roped into helping with many farming tasks. Shirley and Verdon are the most patient of people when instructing most of us on how to do various farming jobs such as fencing, post hole digging, salt bush planting, sheep work etc.

Pam and Geoff, I bet they didn't teach fencing skills at teachers college!

When Verdon travelled, … he was not there like shirley, for the swim up bar and crystal clear water of the pool. He travelled to learn and immerse himself in the history, the religion, geography and the people. Many highlights for us include the family trip around Australia with Shirley, Nanna Hazlett, 2 kids and a 10 foot caravan. Places such as Africa, England, Ireland, Kenya, Germany, France, Hungry, Austria, America and New Zealand. Travelling to India deserves a special mention, because he participated in Sweta's wedding and immersed himself in the religion and experiences that only India can offer.

We can all hold close to our heart the support Verdon has given us all, the love for his wife, children and grandchildren, for the dreams he had for our education and life direction, but mostly for the resilience he tried to instil in all of us….. to be the best that we can be.

So Verdon …… this is not goodbye, but see you later ……… when the Lord unites us all one day ……. and in Verdons own words

"GOD BLESS".

1. Sample Funeral Programs and Templates

A well-structured funeral program provides attendees with an outline of the service while honouring the life of the deceased. Below are examples of typical funeral program formats.

Basic Funeral Program Template

<u>Front Cover:</u>

- Photo of the deceased
- Full name (including any nicknames or maiden names)
- Date of birth – Date of passing
- Funeral service details (location, date, time)
- A short Bible verse or quote (e.g., "The Lord is my shepherd; I shall not want." – Psalm 23:1)

<u>Inside Pages:</u>

Order of Service:

- Opening Prayer
- Scripture Readings
- Eulogy (Given by [Name])
- Tribute Speeches
- Hymns and Songs
- Closing Prayer and Benediction

Obituary Section:

- o A brief life summary including family details, major accomplishments, and notable contributions
- o Personal reflections from family members

Acknowledgments:

- o Thank-you message from the family for support and condolences
- o Mention of pallbearers, clergy, musicians, and any special contributors

Expanded Memorial Program Format

(for those incorporating additional elements)

- o Personal tributes from loved ones
- o Photo collage of memories
- o Favourite prayers, hymns, or poems
- o A donation or memorial request (e.g., "In lieu of flowers, donations may be made to [Charity Name] in memory of [Name].")

2. Public Speaking Tips for First-Time Eulogy Givers

Speaking at a funeral can be an emotional and overwhelming experience, especially for those who are not accustomed to public speaking. Below are key tips to help deliver a eulogy with confidence and composure.

A. Preparing for the Speech

- **Write it out:** Even if you don't read word-for-word, having a structured script or notes will help keep you on track.
- **Practice beforehand:** Read your eulogy aloud multiple times to familiarize yourself with the flow.
- **Time yourself:** A eulogy should typically be between 5–10 minutes.
- **Keep a bottle of water handy:** Pausing for a sip of water can help if you become overwhelmed or emotional.

B. Overcoming Nervousness

- **Take deep breaths before speaking:** This helps regulate nerves and control emotions.
- **Pause when needed:** Don't be afraid to stop for a moment to collect your thoughts.
- **Make eye contact:** If possible, focus on a supportive friend or family member to feel more connected and at ease.
- **Remember why you're speaking:** Your words are a gift to honour the deceased and comfort those in mourning.

C. Handling Emotions While Speaking

- **Acknowledge emotions:** It's okay to show vulnerability. If you tear up, take a moment, breathe, and continue.

- **Have a backup reader:** If emotions become overwhelming, designate someone who can take over if needed.

- **Use a steady pace:** Speaking slowly and clearly will help maintain composure and ensure the audience understands your words.

3. Additional Reading and Grief Support Resources

Grief is a complex process, and seeking guidance from reputable sources can be beneficial for those navigating loss. Below is a curated list of books, online resources, and organizations that offer grief support and education.

A. Books on Grief and Healing

- *A Grief Observed* – C.S. Lewis
- *The Grief Recovery Handbook* – John W. James and Russell Friedman
- *Healing After Loss: Daily Meditations for Working Through Grief* – Martha Whitmore Hickman
- *It's OK That You're Not OK* – Megan Devine
- *When Breath Becomes Air* – Paul Kalanithi

B. Online Grief Support and Counseling

- **GriefShare** – Support groups and daily email encouragement for those in mourning. (https://www.griefshare.org)

- **National Alliance for Grieving Children** – Resources for children experiencing loss. (https://www.childrengrieve.org)

- **The Compassionate Friends** – A community for parents and families grieving the loss of a child. (https://www.compassionatefriends.org)

- **Center for Loss & Life Transition** – Offers educational resources on understanding and coping with grief. (https://www.centerforloss.com)

C. Christian Grief Support Resources

For those seeking a faith-based approach to healing:

- **Grief & Healing Devotionals** – Available through websites like Bible Gateway (https://www.biblegateway.com) and Our Daily Bread (https://odb.org).

- **Church-Based Counseling Services** – Many churches offer grief counseling or support groups.

- **Christian Podcasts on Grief:** – *Ask Grief Coach* (Christian-based grief discussions) *The Bible for Normal People* (Episodes on faith and suffering)

D. Helplines and Immediate Support

If grief feels overwhelming, consider reaching out to a support organization:

- o **Crisis Text Line:** Text HOME to 741741 (24/7 support in the U.S.)
- o **National Suicide Prevention Lifeline:** 988 (U.S.)
- o **SAMHSA's National Helpline:** 1-800-662-HELP (Mental health and substance use disorder resources)

The loss of a loved one is never easy, and navigating the emotions and responsibilities that come with it can be challenging. This section is designed to provide practical resources, speaking guidance, and grief support to help ease the burden and encourage healing.

Whether you are planning a funeral, delivering a eulogy, or seeking comfort in your own grief, know that you are not alone. The power of remembrance, faith, and community will guide you through this journey.

THESAURUS FOR EULOGY WRITING

This section provides a comprehensive list of descriptive words, verbs, and emotions with their synonyms to help readers personalize their eulogies. Thoughtful word choice enhances the emotional depth and sincerity of a eulogy, ensuring that it resonates with the audience while honouring the departed.

1. Verbs (Actions) and Synonyms

Using dynamic and expressive verbs can add clarity and emotion to a eulogy. Below are commonly used verbs and their synonyms to help create a powerful and heartfelt tribute.

Acknowledge – recognize, appreciate, honour, validate, accept, affirm

Break – shatter, disrupt, dissolve, fracture, crack, dismantle

Carry – bear, hold, transport, convey, shoulder, support

Celebrate – commemorate, honour, praise, cherish, rejoice, glorify

Cherish – treasure, adore, value, hold dear, appreciate, revere

Continue – persist, endure, proceed, move forward, persevere, maintain

Dwell – reflect, linger, ponder, contemplate, ruminate, meditate

Encourage – inspire, uplift, support, reassure, motivate, embolden

Express – articulate, convey, declare, reveal, communicate, disclose

Fill – complete, occupy, enrich, satisfy, replenish, imbue

Gather – assemble, collect, unite, congregate, convene, amass

Give – provide, offer, bestow, share, present, donate

Grieve – mourn, lament, weep, sorrow, ache, anguish

Guide – lead, direct, mentor, advise, steer, instruct

Honour – respect, recognize, revere, uphold, venerate, commend

Know – understand, realize, recognize, perceive, comprehend, grasp

Lean – rely, depend, rest, support, incline, tilt

Leave – depart, part, abandon, withdraw, vacate, exit

Lighten – ease, alleviate, brighten, relieve, soften, mitigate

Live – exist, thrive, flourish, persist, endure, survive

Love – adore, cherish, treasure, hold dear, admire, worship

Miss – long for, yearn, mourn, desire, pine for, crave

Offer – provide, present, extend, give, propose, volunteer

Pay – respect, honour, acknowledge, recognize, recompense, tribute

Reflect – ponder, contemplate, consider, meditate, deliberate, muse

Remain – endure, persist, stay, linger, abide, sustain

Remember – recall, honour, reminisce, recollect, retain, recognize

Reunite – reconnect, restore, reconcile, join, assemble, gather

Say – speak, express, voice, articulate, verbalize, proclaim

See – perceive, notice, witness, recognize, discern, observe

Share – express, convey, communicate, distribute, impart, allocate

Show – demonstrate, reveal, present, illustrate, exhibit, portray

Sit – rest, settle, relax, pause, recline, perch

Speak – talk, address, express, communicate, vocalize, enunciate

Support – uphold, assist, encourage, sustain, aid, bolster

Take – accept, embrace, grasp, obtain, acquire, secure

Treasure – cherish, hold dear, prize, value, esteem, safeguard

Value – appreciate, respect, cherish, esteem, honour, admire

2. Emotions & Descriptive Words with Synonyms

Using strong descriptive words enhances the emotional tone of a eulogy. Here is a list of emotions and adjectives with their synonyms to help create a more heartfelt and evocative tribute.

Ache – sorrow, pain, longing, yearning, distress, heartache

Beautiful – lovely, graceful, radiant, exquisite, stunning, breathtaking

Beloved – cherished, treasured, adored, precious, revered, esteemed

Blessed – fortunate, graced, favored, divine, sanctified, gifted

Cherished – adored, beloved, treasured, valued, esteemed, venerated

Comfort – solace, peace, reassurance, relief, tranquility, serenity

Confidant – friend, advisor, supporter, counselor, guide, ally

Courage – bravery, strength, resolve, fortitude, perseverance, resilience

Emptiness – void, loneliness, absence, hollowness, desolation, vacancy

Encouragement – support, reassurance, motivation, inspiration, upliftment, empowerment

Faith – trust, belief, devotion, spirituality, conviction, assurance

Generosity – kindness, selflessness, benevolence, compassion, altruism, magnanimity

Gift – blessing, present, offering, contribution, endowment, legacy

Gratitude – thankfulness, appreciation, recognition, acknowledgment, indebtedness, praise

Grief – sorrow, mourning, anguish, lament, despair, heartbreak

Heavenly – divine, celestial, sacred, eternal, spiritual, blessed

Heavy – burdened, weighted, solemn, intense, grave, oppressive

Honour – reverence, respect, admiration, tribute, commendation, exaltation

Joy – happiness, delight, gladness, elation, jubilation, bliss

Kindness – compassion, warmth, empathy, generosity, goodwill, gentleness

Light – brightness, radiance, glow, illumination, brilliance, shimmer

Love – affection, devotion, adoration, passion, fondness, endearment

Loyalty – dedication, commitment, faithfulness, allegiance, fidelity, devotion

Memories – recollections, remembrances, moments, reflections, impressions, mementos

Missed – absent, longed-for, yearned-for, irreplaceable, departed, lamented

Pain – suffering, anguish, ache, distress, torment, agony

Peace – serenity, tranquility, calm, stillness, harmony, contentment

Presence – existence, being, essence, nearness, proximity, manifestation

Promise – vow, commitment, pledge, assurance, guarantee, covenant

Reflection – contemplation, meditation, introspection, thought, rumination, deliberation

Remembrance – recollection, memory, tribute, homage, commemoration, recognition

Reunion – gathering, coming together, reconnection, restoration, assembly, homecoming

Sadness – sorrow, grief, heartache, melancholy, despair, gloom

Sorrow – mourning, despair, lament, heartbreak, anguish, regret

Strength – resilience, fortitude, determination, perseverance, endurance, vigor

Support – encouragement, aid, help, comfort, backing, reinforcement

Treasured – cherished, valued, held dear, prized, beloved, esteemed

Unwavering – steadfast, resolute, determined, firm, unshakable, unyielding

Value – worth, significance, importance, merit, esteem, appreciation

Wisdom – insight, knowledge, understanding, discernment, prudence, enlightenment

---

> The words we choose when writing a eulogy shape how the deceased is remembered. Selecting powerful, evocative, and heartfelt words ensures that the eulogy is a lasting tribute. This thesaurus serves as a tool to help personalize and enhance sincerity, ensuring every word spoken carries the weight and warmth of remembrance.

Disclaimer: The following "Example Eulogies" are fictional and are provided as examples to assist readers in crafting their own meaningful tributes. Any similarities to real persons, living or deceased, are purely coincidental. These examples are designed to offer guidance, structure, and inspiration for those seeking to honour their loved ones with a heartfelt and well-structured eulogy.

EXAMPLE EULOGIES FOR WRITING GUIDANCE

Alice Parker (Age 8)

Basic Information:

- **Personality Traits:** Energetic, intelligent, humorous, mischievous, deeply curious, and compassionate.

- **Strengths:** Quick learner, strong moral compass, athletic, determined, and deeply empathetic.

- **Weaknesses:** Impatient at times, struggles with losing, occasionally overthinks situations, and can be a little too confident in her abilities.

- **Faith & Spirituality:** Loves attending Sunday School, enjoys listening to Bible stories, and often asks deep, thought-provoking questions about God and the world.

Family & Background:

Alice comes from a loving and supportive family that encourages both her academic pursuits and her energetic passion for sports. She is the middle child in a family of five and often feels like the glue that keeps her older and younger siblings entertained.

- **Mother (Rebecca Parker, 38, Teacher):** A nurturing, patient, and highly intelligent woman who loves books and teaching. She encourages Alice's curiosity and academic excellence, but also tries to teach her the value of patience and humility.

- **Father (James Parker, 40, Firefighter):** A strong yet gentle figure in Alice's life. He is adventurous and always up for a challenge, often playing soccer with her in the backyard or timing her races around the house. He is also the person who reminds Alice to slow down and enjoy the moment.

- **Older Brother (Ethan, 12):** A protective but slightly teasing older brother. He enjoys playing video games and often calls Alice a "little menace" when she outsmarts him in board games. They argue frequently but are inseparable.

- **Younger Sister (Lily, 5):** Alice adores Lily and takes on a big-sister role, though she sometimes finds Lily's constant need for attention exhausting. She loves reading to her and teaching her new things, like how to dribble a soccer ball.

- **Grandmother (Margaret Parker, 67, Retired Nurse):** Alice's spiritual mentor. She shares Bible stories with Alice and helps nurture her faith. Alice enjoys their long walks where they talk about life, faith, and silly things like why clouds look like different animals.

School & Intelligence:

Alice is exceptionally smart for her age. She excels in math and science but has a particular love for storytelling and history. She has a gift for words and often writes short stories in her diary about made-up worlds where she is the hero.

Her teacher, Mrs. Coleman, describes Alice as "a child who could teach the class if she wanted to" but who sometimes gets bored when things move too slowly. She loves solving puzzles, figuring out riddles, and asking questions that even adults struggle to answer.

Friendships & Social Life:

Alice is incredibly social and has a tight-knit group of friends at school and Sunday School.

- **Sophie (8, Best Friend):** Sophie is the more cautious, rule-following friend, balancing Alice's cheekiness. While Alice is always pushing the boundaries, Sophie keeps her in check, often rolling her eyes and saying, "Alice, you're going to get us in trouble!"
- **Jayden (8, Soccer Teammate):** Jayden is Alice's fiercest competitor on the field. He's one of the few kids who can keep up with her energy and wit. They have a playful rivalry, always trying to outdo each other in sports and pranks.
- **Maya (9, Sunday School Friend):** Maya is the deep thinker in their friend group. She and Alice have long conversations about God, the meaning of life, and whether animals go to heaven.

Alice is loved by many but is also a bit of a class clown. She enjoys making people laugh, sometimes at the expense of getting in trouble for speaking out of turn.

Hobbies & Passions:

- **Soccer:** Alice is a natural athlete. She is the fastest runner in her class and plays for her school's soccer team. She dreams of being the best female soccer player in the world one day.
- **Comedy & Acting:** She loves making up stories, acting out funny skits, and pretending to be a stand-up comedian at family gatherings.

- **Reading & Writing:** While she loves physical activity, Alice also has a love for books. She enjoys mystery novels and Bible stories and writes her own short adventures.
- **Sunday School & Faith:** Alice finds deep meaning in her faith. She loves singing hymns, listening to stories of Jesus, and asking **thoughtful questions about** faith that sometimes leave her Sunday School teacher stumped.

Diligent Side vs. Areas for Growth:

Alice is incredibly hardworking in the things she loves. If she sets her mind to winning a soccer game, mastering a math problem, or learning a new trick, she will practice relentlessly. However, if something doesn't interest her, she tends to lose patience quickly and may give up or rush through it.

She also doesn't like losing and can be too competitive, sometimes sulking if she isn't the best at something. Her mother often reminds her that "failure is just practice for success," but Alice isn't convinced yet.

Her cheeky nature is part of her charm, but it can also land her in trouble. She has a knack for saying the funniest thing at the worst time, making her both a joy and a challenge for her teachers.

Future Growth & Potential:

As Alice grows, she has the potential to become an incredible leader, athlete, or even comedian. Her sharp mind, quick wit, and strong moral compass make her someone who could inspire others, but she will need to learn patience and humility along the way.

With the guidance of her faith, family, and friends, Alice will develop into a well-rounded individual who brings joy, curiosity, and boundless energy wherever she goes.

Summary of Alice Parker:

Alice is a spirited, intelligent, funny, and mischievous 8-year-old who excels in sports, loves her faith, and thrives on making others laugh. She has a deep curiosity about the world, an unshakable love for soccer, and a habit of questioning everything. She balances diligence with mischief, excels in what she loves, and is still learning how to navigate patience, humility, and the occasional lesson in losing gracefully.

She is the kind of child who will one day make a difference in the world - whether on the soccer field, the stage, or in the hearts of those she loves.

Eulogy for Alice Parker (Age 8)

Delivered by her father, James Parker

"I never imagined standing here today, speaking words that no parent should ever have to say. My sweet Alice - our bright, beautiful, mischievous, and loving girl - is gone far too soon. There are no words big enough, no sentences strong enough to hold the weight of our grief. But today, I want to honour her. I want to remember her as she was - full of energy, full of laughter, and full of love. Alice was a child who lived every single day as if the world was an adventure waiting just for her." *(Pause)*

"My Alice was unstoppable. From the moment she could walk, she was running - running towards new adventures, new challenges, new experiences. She was the kid who would kick a soccer ball against the house for hours, determined to master her technique. She was the one who couldn't walk past a puzzle without trying to solve it. And she was the one who made sure we all knew when she had outsmarted us at a board game, flashing that cheeky grin and reminding us she was 'the reigning champion of Parker Family Game Night.'" *(Pause to allow smiles and reflections)*

"But more than her competitive spirit, Alice had a heart as big as the sky. She was the kind of child who would stop in the middle of a race just to help a friend who had fallen. She never met a stranger - just future friends she hadn't introduced herself to yet. She loved fiercely, and when she loved you, you knew it. Whether it was the way she hugged her little sister Lily so tightly it almost knocked her over, or the way she defended her older brother Ethan when he got picked on, Alice's love was bold, and it was fierce." *(Pause)*

"My piglet, as I always called her, ran through life at full speed. She never walked when she could run, never whispered when she could shout with excitement, never sat still when she could jump, twirl, or tumble. She was a burst of sunshine in our lives, always keeping us on our toes." *(Pause to let the moment settle)*

"Alice's faith was something special. She loved Sunday School, not just because of the songs or the snacks, but because she was always searching for answers - big, deep, unfiltered questions that made the adults stop and really think. 'Do you think God plays soccer?' she once asked me after a game. And I told her, 'If He does, I think He'd pick you for His team.' That made her smile so big. She truly believed in goodness, in kindness, and in helping others - she was a reflection of everything beautiful that God created in this world." *(Pause, allow the congregation to reflect on her spirit and faith)*

"She was also the funniest person I have ever known. She could light up a room with her laughter, turning even the worst day into something magical. I'll never forget how she used to sneak into the kitchen, steal extra cookies, and then blame the dog - with such conviction that even I started to question whether I had seen her do it. That was Alice - sharp as a tack, full of life, and always keeping us on our toes." *(Pause to let the laughter or warmth settle in the room)*

"Alice was with us for such a short time, and yet, she left us with a lifetime's worth of memories. She taught us what it means to live boldly, to laugh freely, and to love with our whole hearts. Though we don't understand why she had to leave us so soon, we do know this - her light will never go out. It will shine in every story we tell, in every soccer game played in her honour, in every Sunday School question asked by another curious child, and in every time we choose kindness, just as she did."

"We love you, piglet. We miss you more than words can say. And though our hearts are broken, we hold onto the hope that one day, we will see you again. Until then, run fast, play hard, and save us a spot on God's soccer team." *(Long pause to allow the congregation to sit with the words before concluding)*

Alice Parker's eulogy follows a structured format that ensures a heartfelt, engaging, and personal tribute. The opening immediately sets the emotional tone, acknowledging the depth of loss while honouring Alice's vibrant spirit.

The middle section is rich with personal anecdotes, reflecting her personality, passions, and faith, ensuring that the congregation can connect with her essence. Specific stories of her kindness, competitive spirit, and humour bring Alice to life, making the eulogy deeply personal and memorable.

The closing provides comfort and a lasting message, reinforcing Alice's impact and the hope of reunion in faith. Pauses are strategically placed throughout the speech, allowing the congregation to absorb key moments and emotions.

The eulogy also maintains a consistent voice, using her father's first-person perspective and her beloved nickname, Piglet, for added intimacy. This template serves as a model for delivering a meaningful, structured, and emotionally resonant eulogy.

Nathan "Nate" Carter (Age 25)

Basic Information:

- **Nickname:** "Nate" by friends and family
- **Personality Traits:** Charismatic, adventurous, intelligent, humorous, deeply loyal, and full of energy.
- **Strengths:** Quick-witted, highly intelligent, natural leader, deeply compassionate, always the life of the party.
- **Weaknesses:** Struggled with slowing down, always planning his next adventure, could be stubborn when passionate about something.
- **Faith & Spirituality:** Grew up in a Christian home, attended church with his family, and while not deeply religious, he carried a quiet, strong faith that guided his morals and life decisions.

Family & Background:

Nate came from a **large, loving, and tight-knit family** that cherished deep-rooted traditions. His parents worked hard to instill values of **hard work, loyalty, and kindness** in him from an early age.

- **Father (Michael Carter, 52, Construction Manager):** A hardworking, no-nonsense kind of man who had a soft spot for his son's humour and boundless energy. He was immensely proud of Nate's achievements and loved spending weekends watching football and fixing up old cars together.
- **Mother (Rachel Carter, 50, Nurse):** A gentle, nurturing presence in Nate's life. She was his biggest cheerleader,

never missing a soccer game or a school event. Nate always made sure to call his mom first when he had good news.

- o **Younger Sister (Olivia Carter, 21, College Student):** Olivia and Nate were best friends growing up. He was the protective big brother, but also the one who taught her how to drive, how to sneak an extra dessert when their mom wasn't looking, and how to stand up for herself.

- o **Fiancée (Jessica Morgan, 24, Teacher):** Nate and Jessica were high school sweethearts. She was his calm in the storm, the one who balanced his wild ideas with practicality. They had just started planning their wedding when they found out they were expecting their first child - a baby boy Nate was beyond excited to meet.

Education & Career:

Nate had just graduated with a degree in Electrical Engineering, a feat that made his entire family beam with pride. He was brilliant, always the one fixing things, taking apart electronics as a kid just to see how they worked, and designing small gadgets for fun. He had recently secured a high-paying job at a prestigious engineering firm, setting up a bright future for himself, Jessica, and their unborn child.

Despite his intelligence, Nate never let it make him arrogant. He was the guy who could ace an exam but still help his struggling friends study the night before. He was loved not just for his brain but for his heart.

Friendships & Social Life:

Nate had a massive circle of friends. He wasn't just popular - he was deeply loved. His friend group included childhood buddies, university classmates, soccer teammates, and coworkers.

- **Best Friend (Dylan, 25, Fellow Engineer):** They had known each other since kindergarten and were inseparable. Dylan was quieter, more reserved, but Nate always brought out his fun side.

- **The "Second Family" (Jessica's Family):** Jessica's parents adored Nate like a son. He never missed a Sunday dinner at their house and was just as comfortable there as he was in his own home.

- **The Guys (His Soccer Team & College Buddies):** Whether it was playing soccer or hosting backyard BBQs, Nate was the glue that held everyone together. He was the one who planned road trips, the first to crack a joke in tense moments, and the guy who made every night out memorable.

Hobbies & Passions:

- **Soccer:** Nate played semi-competitively, and even though he knew his professional career lay in engineering, soccer **was his passion. He was** known for organizing community matches and coaching kids in his spare time.

- **Fixing Things:** Whether it was a broken toaster, a faulty car engine, or a friend's laptop, Nate could fix anything. His engineering mind was always at work.

- **Adventure & Spontaneity:** Road trips, hiking, camping - if it involved getting out and doing something new, Nate was in. He had a zest for life that was contagious.

- **Family Time:** Despite being constantly on the go, he always made time for Sunday lunch with his parents and breakfast dates with Jessica. Family came first.

The Tragic Accident & Aftermath:

Nate's sudden passing in a car accident left an entire community in mourning. The church was packed beyond capacity, with over 400 people gathered to say goodbye.

Jessica, heavily pregnant with their child, was left devastated but surrounded by love. His parents, sister, friends, and entire community rallied around her, ensuring she never felt alone.

Even in death, Nate left behind a legacy - a child who would carry his name, a fiancée who would always feel his love, and countless friends and family who would never forget his laughter, his kindness, and his unwavering love for life.

Eulogy for Nathan Carter

Delivered by his fiancée, Jessica Morgan

"Standing here today, I still can't believe I'm doing this. I never imagined a world without Nate in it, and I don't want to. He was supposed to be here - to hold my hand, to see the birth of our son, to grow old with me. But somehow, here I am, carrying his child, standing in front of all of you, trying to find words big enough to capture the man we lost." *(Pause for breath and emotion)*

"Nate was more than my fiancé. He was my best friend, my safe place, my home. He was the one who could make me laugh even on my worst days, the one who could fix anything - except this. He could never sit still, always planning the next trip, the next big idea. But no matter what, he always made time for the people he loved."
"Nate had a presence that was larger than life. He could walk into a room, and instantly, you just knew the party had started. His laugh was infectious, his energy unmatched. He was the guy who would stay late to help a friend move, wake up early for a soccer game, and still manage to fix his dad's truck in between." *(Pause to let smiles and emotions settle)*

"He loved his family, his friends, and this crazy, beautiful life. He never took a moment for granted. And he was so excited to be a dad. He would talk to my belly every night, telling our baby boy all the things they were going to do together - teaching him how to play soccer, fixing things in the garage, taking him on camping trips. That's what breaks my heart the most - our son will never get to meet him." *(Pause for emotion, deep breath)*

"But I promise, Nate, I will tell him everything. I will make sure he knows who you were. He will know his father was brilliant, kind, and endlessly loved by so many."

"Nate, I miss you. I miss you in ways I can't even put into words. But I know this - you lived a life that mattered. You loved deeply, you laughed loudly, and you left behind a world that is better because you were in it.

And I know you're still here, in all of us, in our son, in every sunset, in every laugh we share in your memory. Rest easy, my love. Until we meet again." *(Long pause before closing the service)*

Jessica's raw and heartfelt acknowledgment of grief, as she struggles to find the words to express a world without him. Her opening immediately connects with the congregation, drawing them into her sorrow while honouring the man she loved.

The middle section is rich with personal anecdotes that bring Nate's memory to life. His humour, energy, and unwavering love for his family and friends are woven through specific stories that showcase his larger-than-life personality. His passion for fixing things, his dedication to soccer, and his excitement to become a father make the weight of his absence even more profound.

The closing serves as a final tribute, balancing grief with gratitude for the time they had together. Jessica's promise to keep his memory alive through their unborn son offers a sense of hope, reminding everyone that Nate's legacy will continue in the lives of those who loved him.

The eulogy is a model of how to structure a personal and emotionally resonant tribute, one that not only honours the past but carries his spirit forward into the future.

Pamela Carter (Age 52)

Basic Information:

- **Personality Traits:** Strong, nurturing, selfless, determined, loving, resilient, and deeply compassionate.
- **Strengths:** Fiercely protective of her children, a natural caregiver, a hardworking provider, and a woman of quiet but unwavering faith.
- **Weaknesses:** Rarely asked for help, carried too much on her shoulders, struggled with personal rest and self-care.
- **Faith & Spirituality:** A devout Christian who found strength in her faith, she leaned on prayer, scripture, and church community to help her through life's trials.

Family & Background:

Pamela's life was one of **unwavering devotion to her family**. Married to her husband, Mark, for twenty years before his passing, she spent the last decade raising their five children on her own. Despite immense challenges, she never let hardship define her.

- **Husband (Mark Carter, passed away 10 years ago):** Mark was the love of her life. When he died suddenly, Pamela was devastated but resolved to carry on for their children. She always spoke about him with love and made sure his memory was kept alive in their home.
- **Children: Matthew (28, Teacher):** The eldest, a father figure to his siblings, steady and dependable. **Daniel (25, Electrician):** The practical one, hardworking and resourceful like his mother. **Sarah (22, Nursing Student):** The caregiver, deeply empathetic and inspired by Pamela's selflessness. **Emily (19, College Student):** The dreamer,

artistic and full of curiosity. **James (16, High School Student):** The youngest, still growing into himself but shaped by his mother's love.

- **Siblings: Peter (55, Older Brother):** Protective and supportive, always admired Pamela's strength. **Cynthia (50, Younger Sister):** Pamela's confidante and best friend, always there through thick and thin.

Career & Community:

Pamela worked as a hospital administrator, a demanding job that she balanced alongside raising her children. She never let her own exhaustion show, always putting her family's needs first. Beyond work and home, she was deeply involved in her church, where she helped with youth ministry and organized community outreach programs. She was the kind of woman who never turned away someone in need, whether it was a struggling neighbour or a friend going through hard times.

Hobbies & Passions:

- **Faith & Church:** Pamela's faith was her foundation. She attended church every Sunday and was a guiding force in her children's spiritual growth.

- **Cooking:** Known for her legendary Sunday dinners, she brought her family together around the table, no matter how busy life became.

- **Gardening:** She found peace in her garden, planting flowers and vegetables, often saying it reminded her of God's promise of renewal.

- **Writing Letters:** She had a habit of writing heartfelt notes, leaving them in lunchboxes, on mirrors, or tucked into books for her children to find.

The End of Her Journey:

Pamela's sudden passing from a heart attack shocked her family and community. She had always been the strong one, the one who carried everyone else, and in an instant, she was gone. Her children, now grown but forever shaped by her love and sacrifice, gathered to honour the woman who had given them everything.

Peter and Cynthia, her beloved siblings, delivered the eulogy before a congregation of over 300 people - family, friends, colleagues, church members - each of whom had been touched by Pamela's kindness, resilience, and unwavering devotion to others.

Eulogy for Pamela Carter

Delivered by her siblings, Peter and Cynthia

(Peter): "There are no words that could truly capture the depth of Pamela's love, her strength, or the impact she left on all of us. But today, Cynthia and I stand before you, trying to honour our sister the best way we can. Pamela was more than a mother, a sister, a friend - she was the heart of this family, the foundation that held us together." *(Pause for breath, allow emotions to settle)*

"When Mark passed away ten years ago, Pamela could have broken under the weight of that loss. But she didn't. Instead, she rose to meet the challenge - raising five children on her own, working tirelessly to provide for them, and ensuring that their home remained filled with love, laughter, and faith. She never complained, never asked for recognition. She simply did what needed to be done because that's who she was."

(Cynthia): "Pamela was a woman of quiet strength. She never sought the spotlight, but her presence was felt in every act of love she gave. She was the mother who woke up before dawn to make breakfast, the friend who would drop everything to help someone in need, the woman who left notes of encouragement tucked into her children's schoolbooks.

She had a way of making everyone feel special. Whether it was her legendary Sunday dinners, where she made sure no one left hungry, or the simple act of listening without judgment, Pamela had a gift for making people feel seen and loved.

Her faith was her guide, and she lived it not just in words but in actions. She was at church every Sunday, not out of obligation, but because it gave her strength. And she shared that strength with others. She taught her children about grace, about kindness, about the power of resilience. And she lived every one of those lessons herself." *(Pause, allow space for reflection)*

"She loved fiercely, and she was loved just as fiercely in return. She never stopped being a mother, even when her children were grown. Even as adults, they would call her for advice, for comfort, for a reminder that everything was going to be okay."

Peter: "Pamela's love didn't leave when she did. It remains in her children, in her home, in the hearts of every person she touched. It remains in the lessons she taught, in the kindness she gave, in the faith she carried so steadfastly."

Cynthia: "She always said that 'love isn't measured in years, but in moments.' And if that's true, then Pamela lived a thousand lifetimes worth of love. She may not be here physically, but she is with us, in every sunrise, in every prayer, in every memory we cherish."

Peter: "So today, we do not say goodbye. Instead, we say thank you. Thank you, Pamela, for being our sister, our mother, our friend. Thank you for the love you poured into all of us. And thank you for showing us that strength is not in standing alone, but in lifting others up."

Cynthia: "Rest now, dear sister. You have given all you had to give. You have left behind a legacy that will never fade. And though our hearts are heavy, we know we will see you again." *(Pause before concluding the service, allowing time for the congregation to reflect and grieve)*

Pamela Carter's eulogy is a powerful and structured tribute that reflects her unwavering love, strength, and selflessness. The opening immediately acknowledges her role as the heart of the family, setting a tone of both grief and gratitude.

The middle section is rich with personal anecdotes that illustrate her quiet but powerful presence - her selfless devotion to her children, her acts of kindness, and the way she led by example. Strategic pauses allow the congregation to absorb the depth of her impact.

The closing ties everything together with a message of gratitude and faith, ensuring that her legacy of love endures in the lives she touched. This eulogy serves as a model for honouring a devoted mother, a resilient woman, and a guiding light whose presence will never be forgotten.

Harold "Harry" Thompson (Age 65)

Basic Information:

- **Nickname:** Hazard

- **Personality Traits:** Witty, independent, loyal, straightforward, hardworking, and deeply respected.

- **Strengths:** Dedicated community member, reliable friend, natural leader, resourceful, and always the first to lend a hand.

- **Weaknesses (Under Development):** Stubborn, disliked asking for help, never settled down, and had a tendency to keep emotions at arm's length.

- **Faith & Spirituality:** Not a particularly religious man, but believed in fairness, doing the right thing, and helping others whenever he could.

Family & Background:

Harry Thompson was a man who built his own family out of the people around him. Growing up as an only child in a small country town, he learned early on how to be independent. His parents, both hardworking and no-nonsense, raised him with the values of honesty, loyalty, and a strong work ethic. His father was a carpenter, his mother a schoolteacher, and both instilled in him the belief that a man's reputation is only as good as his word. When his parents passed in his early 30s, he found himself without immediate family, but instead of letting loneliness take hold, he threw himself into his friendships, his community, and the clubs he was a part of.

Though he never married and never had children, Harry had a few serious girlfriends over the years. His mates often joked that he was "married to the town," since he spent more time volunteering, organizing events, and being involved in every social club you could name than he did in relationships.

Career & Community Involvement:

Harry worked as a mechanic for over 40 years, running a small auto shop where he knew everyone by name and never charged full price for those who couldn't afford it. He had a rough, dry sense of humour, the kind that made people laugh and shake their heads all at once, but beneath his gruff exterior was a man who would do anything for those around him.

His true legacy was in the community work he did. Over the years, he served as:

- o **President of the Local Rotary Club** – Known for organizing the best charity BBQs and fundraisers.

- o **Volunteer Firefighter** – He might have sworn a lot while on duty, but he was always the first one to show up when someone needed help.

- o **Coach for the Junior Football Club** – Even though he never had kids of his own, he mentored hundreds of young players, teaching them not just about the game, but about character, respect, and resilience.

- o **Lifelong Member of the Town Social Club** – If there was a meeting, Harry was there. If there was a problem, Harry was fixing it.

His friends often joked that he "knew more people than the mayor and probably got more done."

Friendships & Social Life:

Harry's friendships were his chosen family. He surrounded himself with mates from all walks of life, from old work buddies to pub friends to fellow volunteers.

- **Best Friend (Tom, 68, Farmer):** Tom and Harry had been inseparable since they were teenagers. They could sit together for hours in comfortable silence or argue over the same football game for years.

- **The "Social Club Lads"** (Men's Club Members, aged 50-75): A group of old friends who gathered for a beer every Friday night. They all had a "Harry story" to tell - some real, some exaggerated for effect.

- **The Younger Generation:** Though he had no children, Harry was a mentor to many. Young apprentices at his shop, players on the football team, and new volunteers at the fire brigade all looked up to him.

Harry's greatest joy was storytelling. His fabled tales, some true, some gloriously embellished, were best shared over a beer, and anyone who knew him had heard at least one of his legendary adventures.

The End of His Journey:

At 65, Harry finally allowed himself to take a proper holiday with his mates. A fishing trip up north, filled with beers, stories, and endless banter. He had joked for years that he'd "probably go out on a trip like this one day." And, in a way that seemed fitting, he did. He passed away peacefully in his sleep, leaving behind a town full of people who loved him. His funeral was packed with over 300 people, all there to honour the man who had given so much of himself to others.

Eulogy for Harry Thompson

Delivered by his best friend, Tom, and the members of the Social Club

(Tom): "I don't know what Harry would think of all this fuss. He'd probably say, 'What are you all looking at me for? Go back to the pub.' But since he's not here to argue, we're going to do this properly - because a man like Harry Thompson deserves to be remembered." *(Pause, let the room settle)*

"Harry wasn't just my best mate; he was the best mate you could ever have. He had this rough-around-the-edges charm, the kind of guy who would curse at you while fixing your car for free or tell you to 'stop being dramatic' while secretly making sure you were okay. He never married, never had kids, but he had all of us - his mates, his town, his people."

(Rotary Club President): "Harry was the backbone of this town. He ran more fundraisers than I can count, always with his signature scowl - like he was being forced to do it, even though we all knew he lived for it. He had impeccable manners, would never let a lady carry her own bag, but he also had a sense of humour as dry as the Outback."

(Jason,): "When I started working at Harry's shop as a kid, he scared the hell out of me. But I quickly realized that behind all the sarcasm, he cared more than anyone I'd ever met. He taught me everything I know - about cars, about work, about life. He was the father figure I didn't know I needed."

(Tom): "So, what do you say about a man like Harry? You say thank you. Thank you for the stories, for the help, for the laughs, for just being Harry. You say, 'Well done, mate. You lived a life worth remembering.'" *(Pause, raise a beer in his honour)*

"And you go on, telling his stories, sharing his lessons, and making sure his legacy isn't forgotten. That's what he would want. So, here's to you, Harry. May the fish always bite, the beer always be cold, and may we meet again on the other side." *(Long pause before closing the service, allowing the room to reflect.)*

Harry's eulogy is a structured yet informal tribute, mirroring the way he lived - honest, humorous, and full of character. The opening sets the tone, acknowledging his gruff but lovable nature.

The middle is a collection of personal stories, offering glimpses into his generosity, humour, and unwavering dedication to his community.

The closing is a final toast to his memory, celebrating a man who left behind not just a life well-lived, but a legacy of laughter, friendship, and service.

His eulogy serves as a model for honouring someone whose family was the community he built, proving that a man's impact isn't measured in blood relations, but in the lives he touched.

Douglas "Doug" Mitchell (Age 70)

Basic Information:

- o **Personality Traits:** Kind, empathetic, deeply intelligent, diplomatic, and generous.
- o **Strengths:** A brilliant engineer, a dedicated father, a civic-minded leader, and a compassionate soul who always put others before himself.
- o **Weaknesses:** Had difficulty saying no, spread himself too thin, and often put others' needs ahead of his own health and well-being.
- o **Faith & Spirituality:** A private but deeply moral man who lived by the values of kindness, generosity, and humility.

Family & Background:

Doug was born and raised in a small but ambitious town, a place that thrived on community, hard work, and innovation. His parents, both schoolteachers, instilled in him the values of education, curiosity, and public service.

- o **First Marriage:** Doug married young and had three children. Though the marriage ended in divorce, he remained deeply involved in his children's lives and never let the separation diminish his role as a father.
- o **Second Marriage (Titima, 58, Wife of 12 Years):** Later in life, Doug found love again with Titima, a devoted and loving partner from Thailand. She was his rock, his comfort, and his biggest supporter. Their love was deep, patient, and unwavering, and she stood by his side through every chapter of his later years.

Doug's three children were raised with the same kindness, intellect, and work ethic that defined him.

- o **Justin (42, Doctor, Eldest Son):** A dedicated medical professional who lived far away and hadn't seen his father for months before he passed.
- o **Ellen (39, Architect):** A deeply creative spirit who admired her father's engineering mind.
- o **Michael (35, Social Worker):** A community-driven man who inherited Doug's heart for helping others.

Despite physical distance, Doug's love for his children never wavered. He never missed a birthday call and always ended his conversations with "Take care of yourself, and take care of others."

Career & Community Work:

Doug was an engineer of remarkable skill, with a fine engineering degree that allowed him to work on major projects that shaped his town and beyond. His brilliance and problem-solving ability made him sought-after in his field, but his true passion lay in helping others.

In early retirement, Doug dedicated himself to government focus groups, where he provided expert advice on urban planning, infrastructure, and community development. He was respected, admired, and trusted, always using his voice for the betterment of others.

He never turned away someone in need - whether it was mentoring young engineers, helping neighbours with repairs, or giving away his last $5 to a struggling stranger. His generosity was legendary, and his legacy is etched into the community he served.

The End of His Journey:

Doug's passing was unexpected. He had spent the evening talking with Titima about visitors coming to see him in the coming days. He went to bed peacefully, never waking again. The news of his passing sent shockwaves through his family, friends, and the town he loved.

Justin, his eldest son and a doctor, was devastated. Distance and work had kept him away for months, and he struggled with the reality that he never got to say goodbye. But as he prepared to speak at his father's funeral, he knew that his dad's love had never been about proximity - it had been about presence, guidance, and unwavering support.

The funeral was filled with people from every walk of life, from colleagues and government officials to strangers who had once been touched by Doug's generosity. Justin took the podium, ready to honour the father he loved, missed, and would never forget.

Eulogy for Doug Mitchell

Delivered by his eldest son, Justin Mitchell

"There are moments in life that change you forever. Standing here today is one of them. I never imagined I would be speaking at my father's funeral so soon, and I certainly never imagined doing it without having seen him one last time. I regret that distance kept us apart for months, but as I stand before all of you - before this community that he loved - I realize that my father never truly left any of us. His impact is woven into every life he touched, and his legacy is far greater than words can ever express." *(Pause for emotion, allowing the room to settle.)*

"My father was a man of quiet strength. He never raised his voice to prove a point, never sought recognition for the things he did. And yet, he was one of the most influential, compassionate, and giving people I have ever known. He was a man who would give away his last $5 without hesitation, a man who spent his retirement years not resting, but serving."

"My father was an engineer by trade, but he was a builder in every sense of the word. He built bridges - both the physical ones that connected cities and the metaphorical ones that connected people. He built relationships, communities, and opportunities for those who needed them.

He never let anything stop him from helping others. When he retired, he could have relaxed, but instead, he spent his time working with government focus groups, making sure that his town had better roads, safer buildings, and a future for generations to come. He never asked for praise - he just saw a problem and wanted to fix it. That was who he was." *(Pause for reflection, allowing memories to settle.)*

"But the best thing my father built was family. He taught us that love wasn't about distance - it was about showing up in the ways that matter. Whether it was a phone call at the right time, a handwritten letter, or a simple 'I'm proud of you,' my dad made sure we knew he was there."

"My stepmother, Titima, stood by his side every single day, and I know that the love they shared in these past twelve years was the greatest gift life gave him. Dad, if you are listening, please know that she is not alone - we will stand by her the way she stood by you."

"My father was not a perfect man - he was stubborn, he worried too much, and he never knew how to slow down. But if that's the price of being someone who cares too much, then I'd say it's worth it."

"He leaves behind a legacy of kindness, of intelligence, of selflessness. His fingerprints are on the buildings he helped design, the policies he helped shape, and the lives he changed. And though I never got to say goodbye, I realize now that I never had to. Because my father didn't just leave behind memories - he left behind a way to live."

"Dad, I will miss you. I will carry your lessons with me, I will honour your name, and I will make sure that everything you stood for lives on. You were loved. You were admired. And though you are gone, you will never be forgotten." *(Pause, deep breath before concluding the service.)*

Doug's eulogy follows a deeply personal and structured approach, balancing grief with gratitude. The opening addresses regret and distance yet shifts focus to Doug's lasting presence in the lives of those he touched.

The middle section paints a vivid portrait of his character, highlighting his intelligence, generosity, and commitment to others. Justin's words make it clear that his father's impact stretched far beyond their personal relationship - he was a man of the people.

The closing is both emotional and uplifting, reinforcing the idea that Doug's legacy will not fade. It acknowledges his flaws, his strengths, and the deep void he leaves behind, offering a final promise to carry on his work, his love, and his lessons.

This eulogy is a testament to a life well-lived, a man well-loved, and a legacy that will endure beyond his years.

Thank You

To you, the reader, thank you for allowing this book to be part of your journey. Whether you are here in a time of grief, seeking guidance, or preparing to honour a loved one, your willingness to give voice to remembrance is a testament to the love you hold in your heart.

It is never easy to say goodbye, but through words, we keep the memories of our loved ones alive. May you find strength, comfort, and peace as you prepare to share your tribute. May God's grace be with you, and may you always be reminded that love never truly leaves us.

With gratitude and blessings,

Jason A. Solomon

NOTES

THE END

www.ingramcontent.com/pod-product-compliance
Lightning Source LLC
Chambersburg PA
CBHW050558170426
43201CB00011B/1736